FUNDAMENTALS IN BIBLICAL COUNSELING

Equipping Believers to Counsel with Scripture Alone

NICOLAS ELLEN

EXPOSITORY COUNSELING TRAINING CENTER

Publisher's Cataloging in Publication

Ellen, Nicolas*: Fundamentals in Biblical Counseling: Equipping Believers to Counsel with Scripture Alone*

1. Counseling 2. Christian Counseling 3. Christianity 4. Discipleship

Includes bibliographical references

ISBN 978-1-952902-10-9 (paperback)

ISBN 978-1-952902-11-6 (e-book)

Published by Expository Counseling Training Center
Houston, Texas
https://MyCounselingCorner.com

CONTENTS

PREFACE

The Church of Jesus Christ has been entrusted with the sacred responsibility of proclaiming the Word of God and ministering to the souls of men. Counseling, in its truest biblical sense, is not a modern invention but an extension of discipleship—a calling for every believer to walk alongside others with the wisdom of God's Word. In every generation, competing voices arise: psychology built on man's wisdom, integrative models that mix human theories with Scripture, and a growing culture that denies absolute truth. Yet the sufficiency of Scripture stands unchanged. God has given us everything pertaining to life and godliness (2 Peter 1:3), and His Word is the only sure foundation upon which genuine change can be built.

This workbook, *Fundamentals in Biblical Counseling*, seeks to equip believers with a clear framework to minister biblically in the complexities of life. It is written with pastors, leaders, and lay counselors in mind—anyone who desires to counsel with confidence in God's Word alone. The goal is not to train professional therapists but to mobilize disciples who will faithfully "admonish one another" (Rom. 15:14) and help the Body of Christ grow in maturity.

Throughout these pages, you will find a consistent emphasis on God's design for humanity, the reality of sin and suffering, the necessity of heart change, and the hope of the gospel. You will also encounter diagnostic tools, theological foundations, and practical principles that make biblical counseling both doctrinally sound and pastorally effective.

My prayer is that the Lord will use this work to renew your confidence in His Word, deepen your dependence upon His Spirit, and expand your love for His people. May you be equipped to counsel with Scripture alone, pointing others to the only source of true wisdom, healing, and transformation—Jesus Christ.

—Dr. Nicolas Ellen
Expository Counseling Training Center

SECTION 1

The Definition, Goal, and Need of Biblical Counseling

I. The definition and goal of biblical counseling:

Biblical counseling is the personal discipleship ministry of God's people to others under the oversight of God's Church, dependent upon the authority and sufficiency of God's Word through the work of the Holy Spirit. Biblical counseling seeks to reorient disordered thoughts, desires, affections, behaviors, and worship toward a God-designed anthropology in an effort to restore people to a right fellowship with God and others. This is accomplished by speaking the truth in love and applying Scripture to the need of the moment by comforting the suffering and calling sinners to repentance, thus working to make them mature as they abide in Jesus Christ. (Note that this definition, written by Drs. Dale Johnson and Samuel Stephens, was approved by ACBC—the Association of Certified Biblical Counselors.)

A. All good biblical counseling is built around guiding people into knowing God intimately, becoming like Him in character and being useful to Him in service to others by (Col. 1:28):

1. Helping people establish a right relationship with God the Father through putting their faith in the Person and work of Jesus Christ.
2. Helping people understand and address the motivations of their hearts.
3. Helping people put off particular sins that keep them from loving God and loving others.
4. Helping people put on particular patterns of righteousness that produce a love for God and love for others.
5. Providing wisdom to guide people for discerning and choosing the best course of action in a situation.
6. Consoling those who are suffering with biblical understanding and support.

B. Overall, biblical counseling through teaching on and operating by the grace of God is built around helping people (Titus 2:11-15):

1. Gain a biblical understanding of God and submit to God's will accordingly.
2. Gain a biblical understanding of themselves and submit to God's will accordingly.
3. Gain a biblical understanding of others and submit to God's will accordingly.

4. Gain a biblical understanding of life's situations and circumstances and submit to God's will accordingly.
5. Gain a biblical understanding of their calling to serve and submit to God's will accordingly.

II. God has an agenda for saints that includes biblical counseling.

A. God is saving souls from the power, penalty, and soon the presence of sin (Eph. 2:1-10, Col. 1:12-14).
B. God is maturing saints into the image of Jesus Christ (2 Cor. 3:18, Rom. 8:29-30).
C. God is using the Church through evangelism to save souls (2 Cor. 5:18-20, Col. 1:3-6).
D. God is using the Church through discipleship to mature saints into the image of Christ (Matt. 28:18-20, Eph. 4:11-15).
E. Biblical counseling is an avenue whereby evangelism and discipleship can take place, resulting in God using it to save a soul from the power, penalty, and soon presence of sin and maturing saints into the image of Jesus Christ. Every Christian should be involved in evangelism and discipleship. Therefore, every Christian should be a counselor!

III. The problems we encounter in life are the result of the sin of Adam and Eve, which led to the depravity of mankind and the impact of the curse.

A. As a result of Adam's sin, all humans were imputed with sin—placed in the position of sinner before God and considered by position in life a sinner (Rom. 5:12-21, 3:10).
B. As a result of Adam's sin, all of humanity is born with inherited sin—we are born with a heart that is against God; we are born with a sin-infested nature; we are naughty by nature; we are born with a sin condition (Ps. 51:5, Jer. 17:9, Gen. 6:5, Matt. 15:15-20, Rom. 8:7, 7:7-24).
C. As a result of Adam's sin, all of humanity walks in individual sin before God and others (Rom. 3:10-18, 23, 8:5-8; Eccl. 7:20).
D. As a result of Adam's sin, humans experience spiritual death—separation from the influence of God's power, presence, and promises; separation from the indwelling of God in them; separation from fellowship and communication with God; under the control of the devil and his system of living (Eph. 2:1-3).
E. As a result of Adam's sin, humans experience physical death—the spirit of a person is separated from the physical body when physical life ceases (Jas. 2:26).
F. As a result of Adam's sin, humans experience eternal death—separation from God forever after physical death into eternal punishment and damnation (Rev. 20:4-15, John 3:16-18).
G. As a result of Adam's sin, all of humanity tends to worship self and creation above God (Rom. 1:18-32, 2 Tim. 3:1-5, Luke 12:13-21).

H. As a result of Adam's sin, all humans are enemies of God until they come to Jesus Christ for forgiveness of sin and salvation (Rom. 5:10).

I. As a result of Adam's sin, humans in general have become helpless, useless, and slaves to sin apart from salvation in Jesus Christ (Rom. 3:10-18, 8:5-8, 7:7-24).

J. As a result of Adam's sin, humans have sought to set themselves up as autonomous beings, trying to redefine good and evil according to their own standard and to live apart from God (Ps. 14:1-3).

K. As a result of Adam's sin, humans have lost the ability to know themselves accurately (Jer. 17:9).

L. As a result of Adam's sin, humans have lost the ability to judge the universe accurately, making it a god to worship instead of a responsibility to manage (Rom. 1:18-25).

M. As a result of Adam's sin, humans' ability to reason is marred, thereby weakening their ability to discern good and evil (Prov. 14:12).

N. As a result of Adam's sin, humans seek to use people and love things instead of loving people and using things (Rom. 1:18-25).

O. As a result of Adam's sin, imagination has become an illusion, vain and separate from reality (Ps. 73:7).

P. As a result of Adam's sin, humans suffer with creation, with themselves, with others, and with Satan (Gen. 3:17, Rom. 8:20-22, Job 1:19, Luke 13:4-5, Matt. 9:12, Gal. 6:7-8, Ps. 38:1-18, 119:161, 1 Sam. 26:17-25, Luke 22:31).

The Origin of Sin and Suffering

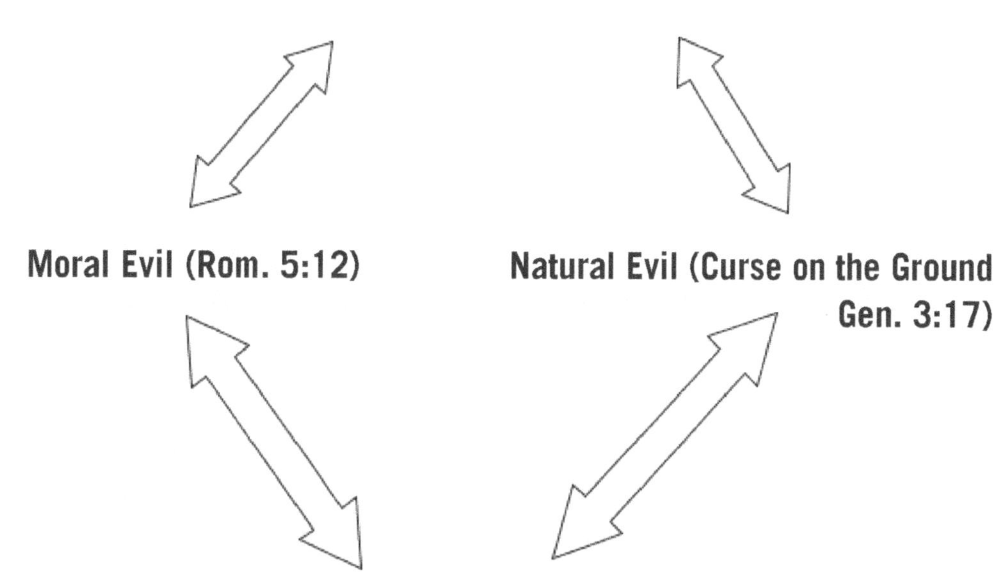

IV. The world seeks to explain away our problems and provide solutions to our problems with ideologies that are inconsistent with the will and ways of God.

Man-Centered Help	God-Centered Help
Helps people to identify and change their mistaken beliefs about self, others, and life, and to participate more fully in a social world.	Helps people identify and change sinful beliefs about self, others, life, and God; Helps them participate in genuine fellowship with God and other Christians as they interact in the world without functioning according to the world's system but by the Word of God (2 Cor. 10:3-5).
Helps people disclose and reevaluate feelings and behavior patterns, to understand and accept previously rejected aspects of themselves to take risks, to become more open and honest about themselves, to learn new methods of living with self and others, and to gain new satisfactions from life.	Helps people to disclose and reevaluate feelings and behavior in light of God's Word in order to learn who each individual is or is not according to God's Word. This is to lead them to put off sinful methods of living and live by righteousness gained by faith in the Person and work of Jesus Christ. This is to result in living for God and enjoying satisfaction gained from living for God (Rom. 12:1-3, Eph. 4:1-32, John 15:1-11).
Focuses on self-efficacy—the individual's belief or expectation that he or she can master a situation and bring about desired change.	Focuses on self-sacrifice: denying self, taking up the cross and following Jesus Christ. People develop the belief that through the power of God, they can be and do all that God commands (Matt. 16:24-26, Phil. 2:12-13).
Takes stock in choosing a direction that best suits a person.	Takes stock in leading a person into choosing God's will in all aspects of life (Col. 1:28-29).
Has the belief system that individuals are the authors of their lives and can design the pathways they want to follow.	Has the belief system that people are created in the image of God and are created for His glory and should therefore submit to God's will and way for their existence (Gen. 1:26-27, Is. 43:7, Col. 1:13-29).
Focuses on significant personality change and adjustment to situational and life problems.	Focuses on transformation of character into the image of Christ in all aspects of life so that people may function to the glory of God and have stability that comes from operating according to the glory of God in life situations (2 Cor. 3:17-4:18, Col. 3:1-25).

V. We need <u>biblical counseling</u> because it is a means by which the issues of life can be addressed at their core level, resulting in using the Scripture to lead individuals into life transformation according to stages of spiritual development. As God is working inside of individuals, they are to respond accordingly (Phil. 2:12-13). Here is an example of how it works (2 Tim. 3:16-17):

A. <u>Teaching Stage</u>**:** The Holy Spirit enlightens people's minds through the Word of God, bringing them into awareness of truth in various aspects of life through the teaching of God's Word. "All Scripture is inspired by God and profitable for teaching."

Biblical counseling uses Scripture to teach them the right way to think, desire, feel, communicate, behave, relate, and serve.

For unbelievers, biblical counseling uses this as an opportunity to show them the reality of God's Word in light of their unbiblical worldview within the context of the issue they brought to the counselor.

B. <u>Conviction Stage</u>**:** God begins to focus one's attention into particular areas of life, convincing people that change is necessary, resulting in conviction, honesty, and godly sorrow through the teaching of God's Word. "All Scripture is inspired by God and profitable . . . for reproof."

Biblical counseling uses the Scriptures to lead people to awareness, conviction, honesty, and brokenness about the sinful thoughts, desires, feelings, communication, behavior, relationship patterns, and serving patterns or lack thereof they tend to have.

For unbelievers, biblical counseling uses this as an opportunity to show them the detriment of sin and their need for our Lord and Savior Jesus Christ within the context of the issues they have brought before the counselor.

C. <u>Correction Stage</u>: As a result of the teaching and conviction from the Word of God, people make a decision to abandon sin issues in their lives. "All Scripture is inspired by God and profitable for . . . correction."

Biblical counseling uses the Scriptures to guide people into putting off sinful thoughts, desires, feelings, communication, behavior, relationship patterns, and serving patterns or lack thereof they tend to have.

For unbelievers, biblical counseling uses this as an opportunity to guide them through the process of repenting and receiving in genuine faith the Person and work of Jesus Christ our Lord to deliver them out of their sin condition into a right standing and right relationship with God.

D. Training Stage: As a result of the teaching and conviction from the Word of God, people put into practice what God has commanded in His Word. "All Scripture is inspired by God and profitable for . . . training in righteousness."

Biblical counseling uses the Scriptures to guide individuals into developing godly thoughts, desires, feelings, communication, behavior, relationship patterns, and serving patterns.

For unbelievers who now have become Christians, biblical counseling uses this as an opportunity to guide them into the basic principles of living out their new life accordingly within the context of the issues they have brought to the counselor and beyond.

VI. We need biblical counseling also because it guides people into how to live life in relation to the pursuit of wisdom for the best course of action (Prov. 1:5, 13:10, 19:20, 27:9). When the unbeliever comes for wisdom, biblical counseling will use the wisdom of God to lead the person back to the gospel of Jesus Christ (1 Cor. 1:21, 25; 2:2-5, 3:18-20).

A. Biblical counseling guides people to direct their *minds* toward a full understanding of human life and toward its moral fulfillment (Elwell and Comfort, 2001).

B. Biblical counseling guides people into the development of their *minds*, an expansion of knowledge, and an understanding of both the meaning of life and how that life must be lived (Elwell and Comfort, 2001).

C. Biblical counseling guides people into the art of being *successful*, of forming the correct plan to gain the desired God-honoring results (Wood and Marshall, 1996).

D. Biblical counseling guides people into the practical skills associated with living a *successful* life. These skills range from the ability to create highly skilled works to the intellectual capability required to make choices that result in favorable outcomes and avoid troubles (Barry, et al., eds., 2016).

E. Biblical counseling guides people into factual knowledge, the situational insight, and the necessary resolve that together have the greatest likelihood of *success* in achieving the intended, righteous goal (Piper, 2018).

VII. In addition, we need <u>biblical counseling</u> to provide support, encouragement, and guidance through difficulties of life, those not created by the person, by focusing on the support and sanctification of Christians and the support and salvation of unbelievers (1 Thess. 5:14).

A. If people are suffering from *situations beyond their control,* counseling guides people to worship God as they grieve over suffering while accepting the sovereignty of God over their lives by working through the matter with endurance; pursuing wisdom to fix, resolve, or work through the matter (Job 1:19-20, Eccl. 7:13-14, 9:1, Jas. 1:1-5, Rom. 12:15). (Presenting support and the gospel to unbelievers).

B. If people are suffering from *sickness,* counseling guides people to pray for help, to repent of sin if there be any tied to the sickness, and to trust in the Lord and function in obedience in spite of their sickness (Jas. 5:13-15, Prov. 3:5-8). (Presenting support and the gospel to unbelievers).

C. If people are suffering from the *sin of others,* counseling guides people to embrace the reality that what others meant for evil, God will use to bring good to their lives while obeying God in spite of the sin of others. Where appropriate, counseling will guide people to confront others about the sin (Gen. 50:20, Rom. 8:28, 12:17-21, Luke 17:3, Gal. 6:1). (Presenting support and the gospel to unbelievers).

D. If people are suffering from *Satan,* counseling guides people to submit to God and resist the devil with the spiritual armor given to them by God, which will cause the devil to flee from them (Jas. 4:7, Eph. 6:13-17). (Presenting support and the gospel to unbelievers).

E. If people are suffering from *serving,* counseling guides people to embrace the fact that God will provide comfort in the midst of their affliction while continuing to serve, which will result in developing in endurance and lead to Christ-like character being developed (2 Cor. 1:1-7, Jas. 1:1-4). (Presenting support and the gospel to unbelievers).

The revelation of Jesus Christ creates a distinctive conception of the relationship between counselor and counselee, a distinctive understanding of methodology, a distinctive social location for a counseling practice to flourish. This care and cure for the soul systematically differs from how other psychotherapies deal with the same problems in living. Nothing comes ready-made. Biblical counseling wisdom is an ongoing construction project, like all practical theological work. It is one outworking of biblical faith into the particulars of our time, place, problems and persons (Powlison, 2010, 245).

SECTION 2

What Makes Biblical Counseling Biblical?

Three Major Schools of Thoughts in Counseling

Psychological Counseling—combines human observations with human wisdom to construct a system of counseling to help people deal with their problems and issues of life. This type of counseling is generally practiced by nonbelievers and Christians who accept psychological theories as an avenue to help people.

Integration Counseling—combines human observation, human wisdom, and the Bible to construct a system of counseling to help people deal with their problems and issues of life. This is sometimes called "Christian Counseling." This type of counseling is generally practiced by Christians who believe the Bible should be supplemented with psychological theories in order to help people.

Biblical Counseling—uses the Bible to construct a system of counseling to help people deal with their non-physical or immaterial problems of life. This type of counseling is generally practiced by Christians who believe that the Bible has all we need to provide solutions to people's non-physical or immaterial problems. as well as what the world calls "psychological" problems. They also believe that the Bible can help people function as God intended in life.

A Description of Biblical: Biblical counseling can be described as using the Word of God (the Bible) within the context it was written to provide solutions and the application of those solutions to non-organic, immaterial, spiritual, and what the world calls "psychological" or "mental disorder" problems. The Word of God is used in a precise and efficient manner to address these matters. The Word of God is used in anticipation of the salvation of sinners and the sanctification of saints as a result. Biblical counseling can also be defined as using the Word of God to give comprehensive answers to non-physical problems on a small-group level or one-on-one interpersonal level. In essence, biblical counseling is applied biblical systematic theology. It is the practical ministry that comes out of knowing and understanding the Bible and the theology of the Bible. Biblical counseling is the practical, comprehensive ministry of soul care that comes out of knowing, understanding, and applying biblical systematic theology to life issues.

I. Logical implications of biblical counseling

A. God is saving souls from the power, penalty, and soon the presence of sin (Eph. 2:1-10, Col. 1:12-14).

B. God is maturing saints into the image of Jesus Christ (2 Cor. 3:18, Rom. 8:29-30).

C. God is using the Church through evangelism to save souls (2 Cor. 5:18-20, Col. 1:3-6).

D. God is using the Church through discipleship to mature saints into the image of Christ (Matt. 28:18-20, Eph. 4:11-15).

E. Biblical counseling is an avenue whereby evangelism and discipleship can take place, resulting in God using it to save a soul from the power, penalty, and soon presence of sin and maturing saints into the image of Jesus Christ. Every Christian should be involved in evangelism and discipleship. Therefore, every Christian should be a counselor!

1. Biblical counseling focuses on helping people deal with the heart issues that drive their behavioral issues, as explained by God in His Word (Jas. 3:13-4:10, Luke 6:43-45, Matt. 6:19-21, Ezek. 14:1-11).
2. Biblical counseling focuses on helping people turn from sin in their thoughts, words, actions, and relationships, as prescribed by God in His Word (Col. 3:5-9, Eph. 4:17-22, 1 John 1:9, Prov. 28:13-14).
3. Biblical counseling focuses on helping people walk in Christ's righteousness in their thoughts, words, actions, and relationships, as prescribed by God in His Word (Gal. 5:16-25, Eph. 4:23-32, Col. 3:10-25, Rom 12:1-3).
4. Biblical counseling facilitates the process of individuals becoming like Christ in all aspects of life (Eph. 4:11-16, Col. 1:28-29).
5. Biblical counseling leads a person into truth that comes from God and not human observations and theories that are an antithesis to Scripture (Matt. 28:18-20, 1 Tim. 6:3-6, 2 Peter 1:16-21).
6. Biblical counseling leads unbelievers to Christ as it shares with unbelievers their ultimate problem (sin) and their true need of salvation (2 Cor. 5:15-21).
7. Biblical counseling helps individuals in the Body of Christ grow spiritually as it focuses on their real problem—sin—and their solution: putting off sin and putting on righteousness (Eph. 4:17-32, 2 Peter 1:1-10).
8. Biblical counseling provides the community with God's solutions to life's immaterial, non-physical, or what the world calls "psychological" problems (Col. 1:28-29).
9. Biblical counseling depends on the sufficiency of Scripture instead of human traditions and theories (Col. 2:8-9, 2 Tim. 3:16-17, Ps. 1:1-2, 19:7-11).

10. Biblical counseling is rooted and grounded in a worldview that all things are from God, through God, and to God. Therefore, all things must be evaluated from His perspective (Rom. 11:36). Questions such as the following are addressed through God and His Word.

    a. What is the nature of humans, and what is their relationship to God?
    b. What is humanity's fundamental problem?
    c. How should we and how do we relate to our fellow human beings?
    d. What values should guide and what values do guide our attitudes and actions?
    e. How can people solve their basic problems?
    f. What specific changes should they make?
    g. Who/what is the agent for such change?
    h. What are the goals of these changes?

11. True biblical counseling will demonstrate:

    a. A high view of God in His character, nature, attributes, etc.
    b. A high view of the sufficiency of Scripture.
    c. An accurate anthropology (humans are basically evil and in need of salvation/ sanctification).
    d. A biblical understanding of the purpose of the Church.
    e. A biblical view of Church leadership.
    f. Insight that is based on biblical foundations.
    g. Methodologies that are based on biblical foundations.
    h. Goals that are God-centered instead of human centered.

Concept I—insights gained in teachings from Dr. Lance Quinn

II. Helpful quotations about <u>biblical counseling</u>

A. "The information unbelievers come to know by God's common grace is simply not as important for counseling as the truth God reveals in the Bible about how Jesus changes people. Troubled people can know much information about counseling through common grace, but what they most deeply need is the Bible to reveal Jesus and his special grace in salvation" (Lambert, 2016, 101).

B. "When biblical counselors do their work, they are engaging in a conversation about the questions, problems, and troubles of their counselee and seeking to offer answers, solutions, and help. All manner of information may be true and available to a counselor that is not relevant for the answers, solutions, and help offered in counseling.... The issue is not the existence and importance of extra-biblical information made possible by the means of God's common grace. The issue concerns the nature of central information vital to a task, such as counseling, versus peripheral information" (Lambert, 2016, 96-97).

C. "When biblical counselors emphasize the use of Scripture to the exclusion of other resources, it is not a denial that accurate information is available in other places. It is a statement that no other source of information, no matter how true, offers the kind of help for counseling that God does in his Word" (Lambert, 2016, 84).
D. "Scripture alone is sufficient for life and godliness. That does not mean it contains all truth, but that it contains all the truth necessary for what God desires us to be and do" (Adams, 1970, 56).
E. "Counseling is not simply about making people feel better, but about making people more like Christ" (Lambert, 2011, 32).
F. "Counseling that is biblical will not be satisfied with a man-centered agenda but will be driven by a God-centered purpose" (Powlison, 2005, 25).
G. "The gospel is not just the entry point to Christianity; it is the very framework for counseling and change" (Piper, 2005, 11).
H. "If you think of people as basically good, you will counsel them differently than if you think of people as fallen sinners. Biblical counseling starts with a biblical anthropology" (MacArthur and Mack, 2005, 21).
I. "True change is not accomplished by human effort alone. It is wrought by the Spirit of God applying the Word of God to the hearts of the people of God" (Tripp, 2002, 78).
J. "Counseling is intensely practical. The goal is not simply to impart biblical truth but to equip people to live it" (Mack, 1979, 9).

Key Point: Your view of counseling will be determined by your worldview. The more biblical your worldview, the more biblical your counseling. The less biblical your worldview, the less biblical your counseling will be. Your worldview is determined by those whom you have allowed to teach you. The Bible says, "No student is greater than his teacher, but a fully trained student will be like his teacher" (Luke 6:40, NCB). You must determine if your view of counseling has been shaped by teaching that is driven by Satan or teaching that is driven by the Son of God! In other words, you must evaluate your model of counseling to determine if it is biblical or unbiblical.

III. Sixteen key questions to evaluate any counseling model

A. According to this model, what is the assumption about the existence of God, His rule, and His role in relation to creation and to humanity?

B. According to this model, what is the belief about of the nature of humans (just body and brain with no spiritual dimension / both physical and spiritual dimension)?

C. According to this model, what is humanity's basic problem?

D. According to this model, what do humans need to resolve their problem to become whole?

E. According to this model, what is the process (methodology) of providing humans what they need in order to resolve their problem to become whole?

F. According to this model, what is the evidence that a person has resolved his/her problem and become a healthy / whole human being?

G. What does this model lead people to do in relation to thoughts, words, or deeds?

H. What does this model lead people to become in character?

I. What kingdom does this model represent overall, God's Kingdom or Satan's kingdom? Explain.

J. How does this model compare or contrast with the doctrines of God, creation, humanity, sin, suffering, salvation, and sanctification as explained in the Bible?

K. What are the biblical scriptures and principles that support or refute this model?

L. What is this model's primary source of knowledge: empirical research, Scripture and theology, philosophy, personal experience, or history?

M. How accepting or distrusting is this model in the embracing of contemporary counseling/psychology?

N. Is the goal of this model to pursue a distinctive understanding of human nature, to which only Christians would subscribe, or a universal understanding that all psychologists and counselors, regardless of their worldview, can recognize and affirm?

O. Is this model's primary allegiance to the Church or the broader community of scholars and practitioners in the culture?

P. Is the model's primary task the acquisition of knowledge about human beings, or the renovation of human beings according to God / not according to God, or the cultivation of godliness, moral character, and love?

Questions L–P influenced by Johnson, 2010, 40

SECTION 3

Secular and Integration Theories

I. The difference between secular, integration, and biblical models of counseling

A. ***Psychological Counseling***—combines human observations with human wisdom to construct a system of counsel to help people deal with their problems and issues of life. This type of counseling is generally practiced by non-believers and Christians who accept psychological theories as an avenue to help people.

B. ***Integration Counseling***—combines human observation, human wisdom, and the Bible to construct a system of counsel to help people deal with their problems and issues of life. This is sometimes called "Christian counseling." This type of counseling is generally practiced by Christians who believe that the Bible should be supplemented with psychological theories in order to help people.

C. ***Biblical Counseling***—takes the Bible to construct a system of counsel to help people deal with their problems and issues of life. This type of counseling is generally practiced by Christians who believe that the Bible has all we need to provide solutions to life's non organic, immaterial, and what the world calls "psychological problems" and to help people function as God intended in all aspects of life.

II. **Understanding the foundations for psychological counseling:** Modern psychology rests on a distinctly *human-centered* foundation. Its assumptions shape how it defines problems and proposes solutions.

A. Within the framework of modern psychology, the central task is not to give answers, but to *help clients discover solutions that fit their personal values* (Corey, 2016, 7).

B. Counseling aims to help clients clarify their own values, define personal goals, make autonomous decisions, and assume responsibility for outcomes (Corey, 2016, 8).

C. According to the American Counseling Association's 2014 Code of Ethics, counselors must avoid imposing values and must respect the diversity of the client's worldview (ACA, 2014; cited in Corey, 2016, p. 14).

D. Counselors must practice within the client's value commitments; if a conflict arises, the counselor must seek training and supervision to manage ethical tensions (Corey, 2016, p. 15).

E. Historically, "counseling" was associated with practical problem-solving by less formally trained helpers (e.g., pastors, school counselors), while "psychotherapy" addressed personality change and deeper internal issues, led by highly trained professionals (Jones, 2010). Over time, counseling and psychotherapy have become more similar and their boundaries nearly indistinguishable. Historically, doctoral-level practitioners have distinguished between *counseling* and *psychotherapy*.

III. Understanding the foundations of integration counseling: The integration movement emerged as evangelicals attempted to maintain fidelity to Scripture while embracing psychological theories and methods.

A. In 1952, Hildreth Cross introduced psychology through an evangelical lens, seeking to maintain scriptural authority while presenting psychological concepts (Johnson, 2010, 31).

B. Christian psychologists formed the *Christian Association for Psychological Studies (CAPS)* in 1956 to explore how Christian faith could intersect with psychology (Johnson, 2010, 32).

C. Clyde Narramore and Paul Tournier popularized a Christian-friendly psychology through radio, books, and translated works. Their writings married Christian themes with ideas from Rogers, Freud, and Jung, providing evangelicals with psychologically informed approaches (Johnson, 2010, 33-34).

D. By the mid-1960s, major institutions such as Fuller and Rosemead established doctoral programs blending psychology and theology. Journals like the *Journal of Psychology and Theology* and *Journal of Psychology and Christianity* emerged to support integration (Johnson, 2010, 35- 37).

E. In the 1970s well-known Christian authors such as Collins, Dobson, and Narramore further promoted psychological concepts—self-esteem, personality theories, and therapeutic methods—in Christian circles (Johnson, 2010, 38).

F. Integrationists argue that psychology and Christianity offer complementary truths that, when combined, help produce a more complete understanding of the person (Boereê, 2011). They also assert that counselors should borrow techniques from secular theories if filtered through Scripture. Critics argue that psychology is built on secular humanism. Many of its presuppositions conflict with biblical anthropology. Attempts to merge these systems ultimately distort the sufficiency of Scripture (Johnson, 2010, p. 39; Kim, 2012).

IV. The difference between descriptive data and prescriptive data

A. **Descriptive vs. Prescriptive Analytics:** Descriptive data recount what has happened (patterns, history, tendencies). Prescriptive data recommend what should be done (action steps, solutions, strategies).

B. **Application to Counseling:** Descriptive data can identify patterns about a person or situation. But nonbiblical sources often interpret data through unbiblical philosophies. Prescriptive data are even more dangerous because they tell us *how* to live. Scripture warns against being *taken captive by human philosophy* (Col. 2:8). Therefore, descriptive data must be evaluated by Scripture, and prescriptive data must be rejected unless it aligns fully with biblical truth.

V. The definition of general revelation (Rom. 1:18-21, 2:14-15)

A. God's disclosure of Himself to the entire world at *all times and places*.

B. God's disclosure of Himself to the entire world at all times and places through *nature*.

C. God's disclosure of Himself to the entire world at all times and places through *history*.

D. God's disclosure of Himself to the entire world at all times and places through human *conscience*.

E. God's disclosure of Himself to the entire world at all times and places through *work of the law written on people's hearts*.

VI. What does God disclose about Himself through general revelation? (Rom. 1:18-21, 2:14-15)

A. Through general revelation, God discloses His *invisible attributes*.

B. Through general revelation, God discloses His *eternal power*.

C. Through general revelation, God discloses His *divine nature*.

D. Through general revelation, God discloses His *divine moral code*.

VII. What are the implications of general revelation for humanity? (Rom. 1:18-21, 2:14-15)

A. Through general revelation, humans have come to understand that *God exists*.

B. Through general revelation, humans have come to understand that *God exists with divine character and divine power.*

C. Through general revelation, humans have come to understand that *God has a divine moral code by which people are to operate.*
D. Through general revelation, humans have *no excuse for their rejection of God*.

VIII. The definition of special revelation (Acts 10:1-48, Gen. 12:1-7, Heb. 1:1-2, John 8:31-32, 1 Thess. 1:1-10)

A. God's *manifestation of Himself* to particular persons at definite times and places, *enabling those persons to enter into a redemptive relationship with Him* (Erickson, 1998, 175)
B. God's *manifestation of Himself through dreams and visions* to particular persons at definite times and places, *enabling those persons to enter into a redemptive relationship with Him*
C. God's *manifestation of Himself through the angelic appearances(theophanies) and angels* to particular persons at definite times and places, *enabling those persons to enter into a redemptive relationship with Him*
D. God's *manifestation of Himself through prophets* to particular persons at definite times and places, *enabling those persons to enter into a redemptive relationship with Him*
E. God's *manifestation of Himself through a voice from heaven, incarnation, and the inspired Word of God* to particular persons at definite times and places, *enabling those persons to enter into a redemptive relationship with Him*

IX. God's special revelation is now summed up in the Word of God (2 Peter 1:16-21, 2 Tim. 3:16).

A. God uses His Word/Scriptures to guide us into the way we are to relate with God, others, ourselves, the world, and even our circumstances (Ps. 19:7-11, 119:1-16, Prov. 30:5-6, Is. 55:6-11).
B. God uses His Word to enlighten us to truth, to convict us of sin, to guide us into correcting wrong, to guide us into training in what is right according to Him (2 Tim. 3:16).
C. God uses His Word to train us into discerning good from evil (Heb. 5:12-14).
D. We cannot know the will of God without the Word of God (Rom. 12:2, Ps. 1:1-3, John 8:31-32).

X. Implications of general and special revelation

A. Through general revelation you come to learn that God exists (Rom. 1:18-20).
B. Through special revelation you come into a redemptive relationship with God (John 8:31-32).

C. Through general revelation you come to learn that God exists and has standards by which you are to operate (Rom. 1:18-20, 2:14-15).
D. Through special revelation you learn how to relate with God and how to function in accordance with His will, experiencing restoration and transformation (Ps. 19:7-11).

XI. Implications for biblical counseling

A. Unbelievers have suppressed the truth in unrighteousness. Therefore, all apologetics or challenging of their debate or denial of the existence of God should eventually lead to presenting the gospel of Jesus Christ when counseling (special revelation).
B. Do not give unbelievers truths to follow without giving them Christ to surrender to first. They need to surrender to a Person, not follow a concept. Our counseling should emphasize this reality (special revelation).
C. Believers have a need to engage in the all-sufficient Scripture for the sake of true spiritual growth. Therefore, our counsel must be through the Word of God (special revelation).
D. Insights for living a quality life will not come through general revelation but through special revelation. Therefore, our counsel should be through the Word of God (special revelation).

The Nature of Truth (Is all truth God's truth?)

The Bible gives us all we need for *mental soundness* and for understanding and dealing with the basic needs of the *inner, immaterial man.* God's Word instructs us to find from Scripture alone our principles for living; our understanding of human attitudes, motives, behaviors; and our solutions for man's non-organic, immaterial, inner problems and what the world calls *psychological problems* (Col. 2:8, Ps. 1:1-3, Rom. 12:2-3).

"All truth is God's truth." However, people can easily deceive themselves and should not trust their own assessments. We need truth revealed from the One Who knows all truth in order to be sure human "truth" is actually truth (John 14:26, 16:13, 17:17, Prov. 3:5-6, 2 Cor. 12:12, Heb. 2:3-4, Mark 16: 17-20). When Scripture acknowledges our observations about ourselves as true, it is saying simply that our observations must be included in the Bible in order for us to know that the observations are true (Ps. 1:1-2, Col. 2:8, Prov. 3:5-6, 14:12, 16:25, 24:30-34, Jer. 17:9, Is. 55:8-11). Also applicable are First Corinthians 15:33 (written by Menander, a playwright, and confirmed as true by Scripture); Acts 17:28 (written by a poet but confirmed as true by Scripture); and Titus 1:12-13 (referenced a pagan prophet but confirmed as true by Scripture).

Israel took the physical gold, silver, and jewels, and were warned not to copy their philosophy of life from the Egyptians. God was seeking to change their philosophy. Believers are not to take the philosophy of life that comes from the world (Ps. 1:1-2, Col. 2:8).

The Nature of Truth information is gleaned from Thomson, 2012.

Conclusion: Secular counseling begins with human wisdom and centers on the client's values. Integration counseling attempts to merge psychological theories with Scripture, but in practice often elevates human insight to a level that weakens biblical authority. Biblical counseling stands apart because it begins and ends with special revelation—the sufficient, inerrant Word of God. Unlike secular and integration models, biblical counseling recognizes that true understanding of the inner person and true transformation of the heart can only come through Scripture. For believers, no other method offers God's wisdom, God's diagnosis, or God's solutions. Therefore, biblical counseling is the only model that aligns fully with God's revelation and leads people toward Christlikeness, obedience, and lasting spiritual change.

SECTION 4

Qualifications of a Biblical Counselor

I. A biblical counselor should be one who is *guarded* and governed by the Holy Spirit, thus displaying the fruits of the Holy Spirit in attitudes, values, words, and actions (Gal. 6:1).

II. A biblical counselor should be one who is aware and *honest* about his own sinful tendencies and character flaws, seeking to deal with them accordingly (Gal. 6:1).

III. A biblical counselor should be one who ministers by the *Word of God* and does not use any theories or practices that contradict or violate God's standards (2 Tim. 4:1-5).

IV. A biblical counselor should be one who seeks to help others recover from the consequences of *poor decisions* (Gal. 6:2).

V. A biblical counselor should be one who seeks to help others *confess* and *repent* of sin (Gal. 6:1-2).

VI. A biblical counselor should be one who seeks to help others function in *spiritual maturity* in all aspects of life (Eph. 4:11-16).

VII. A biblical counselor should be one who seeks to hold others *accountable* to stay away from people, places, and products that will lead them into sin (Heb. 3:12-13).

VIII. A biblical counselor should be one who seeks to stimulate others to *love* and *good deeds* (Heb. 10:19-25).

IX. A biblical counselor should be one who is not *quarrelsome* but *kind* to all (2 Tim. 2:24).

X. A biblical counselor should be one who is able to teach others the *truth of God's Word* (2 Tim. 2:24).

XI. A biblical counselor should be one who is able to *practice patience* when others are mistreating her or him (2 Tim. 2:24).

XII. A biblical counselor should be one who is able to *gently correct* those who are in *opposition* to the truth (2 Tim. 2:25).

XIII. A biblical counselor should be one who *builds up* others with his/her *words* (Eph. 4:29).

XIV. A biblical counselor is committed to development in:

A. Character—to reflect the personality of God on the inside and outside.
"That in reference to your former manner of life, you lay aside the old self, which is being corrupted in accordance with the lusts of deceit, and that you be renewed in the spirit of your mind, and put on the new self, which in the likeness of God has been created in righteousness and holiness of truth" (Eph. 4: 22-24).

B. Conduct—to carry him- or herself in a manner that represents the holiness of God and not self-righteousness or self-indulgence.
"As obedient children, do not be conformed to the former lusts which were yours in your ignorance, but like the Holy One who called you, be holy yourselves also in all your behavior, because it is written 'You shall be Holy for I Am Holy'" (1 Peter 1:14-16).

"Therefore if you have been raised up with Christ, keep seeking the things above, where Christ is seated at the right hand of God. Set your mind on things above, not on the things that are on the earth" (Col. 3:1-2).

C. Conversation—to speak words and to have dialogue that displays the character of God.
"Let no unwholesome word proceed from your mouth, but only such a word as is good for edification according to the need of the moment, so that it will give grace to those who hear" (Eph. 4:29).

D. Commitments—devoting her- or himself to God.

"Therefore I urge you, brethren, by the mercies of God, to present your bodies a living and holy sacrifice, acceptable to God, which is your spiritual service of worship" (Rom. 12:1).

"Go therefore and make disciples of all the nations, baptizing them in the name of the Father and the Son and the Holy Spirit, teaching them to observe all that I commanded you; and lo, I am with you always, even to the end of the age" (Matt. 28:19-20).

E. Commodities—enjoying and sharing generously the resources God has provided him or her, without putting hope in the resources God has provided.

"Instruct those who are rich in this present world not to be conceited or to fix their hope on the uncertainty of riches, but on God, who richly supplies us with all things to enjoy. Instruct them to do good, to be rich in good works, to be generous and ready to share" (1 Tim. 6:17-18).

F. Communion—staying in consistent fellowship with other believers.

"And let us consider how to stimulate one another to love and good deeds, not forsaking our own assembling together, as is the habit of some, but encouraging one another; and all the more as you see the day drawing near" (Heb. 10:24-25).

XV. A biblical counselor is committed to:

A. seeking the *highest of good* of others unconditionally, no strings attached, to accomplish God's intended goals for others.

B. responding to the *condition and need* of others, above the attractiveness and personal interest in others, to accomplish God's intended goals for others.

C. having a *genuine concern* and *benevolence* toward others to accomplish God's intended goals for others.

D. having a *selfless service* and *sacrifice* of his or her life for the sake of others to accomplish God's intended goals for others.

SECTION 5

The Process of Biblical Change

I. The <u>position</u> and <u>power</u> of change

A. Because of our union with Christ, we have the power to walk in the newness of life with God (Rom. 6:1-14).
B. Because of the indwelling Holy Spirit, we have the power to change and reflect the character of Jesus Christ in our lives (Rom. 8:1-13).
C. As new creatures in Christ, we can live reconciled lives to God while walking in the ministry of reconciliation to others (2 Cor. 5:17-21).
D. In summary, because of our position in Christ and the power of the Holy Spirit who indwells, we have the ability to change and reflect the image of Jesus Christ.

II. The <u>premise</u> of change

A. To help people establish a right relationship with God the Father through our Lord Jesus Christ (2 Cor. 5:20-21).
B. To help people put off particular sins that keep them from loving God and loving others (Eph. 4:17-32).
C. To help people put on attitudes and actions of love for God and others, which should lead to becoming like Christ in all things (Phil. 2:1-8).
D. To help people grow in wisdom in areas of preference (Rom. 14:1-23).

III. The <u>points</u> of change

A. People will need to change in thoughts, attitudes, motives, and desires (Rom. 12:2, Phil. 2:4, Col. 3:1-2).
B. People will need to change in conversations and communication (Eph. 4:29).
C. People will need to change in behavior and lifestyle (Col. 3:5-11).
D. People will need to change in how they relate to others as well as serve God and others (Col. 3:12-16, Gal. 5:6,13, Rom. 12:3-21).

IV. The parameters of change (Rom. 12:2)

A. People will need gain a biblical understanding of God and submit to His will accordingly.
B. People will need to gain a biblical understanding of themselves and submit to God's will accordingly.
C. People will need to gain a biblical understanding of others and submit to God's will accordingly.
D. People will need to gain a biblical understanding of life's situations and circumstances and submit to God's will accordingly.

V. The people of change

A. Genuine disciples of Jesus Christ listen to the truth of God's Word and seek to make changes accordingly (John 8:31-32).
B. Genuine disciples of Jesus Christ listen to the truth of God's Word and seek to make changes with the ultimate goal of becoming like Jesus Christ (1 John 3:1-24).
C. Genuine disciples of Jesus Christ listen to the truth of God's Word and seek to make changes with the intent of helping others make the changes as well (John 13:1-17).
D. Genuine disciples of Jesus Christ listen to the truth of God's Word and seek to make changes with the ultimate goal of seeking to know God intimately (Phil. 3:1-21).

VI. The picture of change

A. Genuine disciples of Jesus Christ tend to evaluate things from a biblical perspective (Heb. 5:13-14, Jas. 3:13-17).
B. They tend to reflect the lifestyle of Christ (Gal. 5:16-23, 2 Peter 1:1-10).
C. They tend to share the gospel consistently (2 Cor. 5:17-20).
D. They tend to serve using their gift(s), producing positive results (1 Peter 4:10-11, John 15:1-5, Luke 6:43-45).

VII. The personalities encountered in change

Based on ideas from Adams, 1985, ch. 2

A. Those who *lack knowledge*, yet once they receive it are able to work on their problems and honor God.
B. Those who *have knowledge* but don't know how to apply it to their problems and honor God.

C. Those who *have knowledge* and *have skill* to apply their knowledge but *refuse to apply* what they know to work on their problems and honor God.
D. Those who *lack knowledge* and are not interested in getting knowledge or skill to work on their problems and honor God.

VIII. The problems that hinder change

A. Consistently yielding to the tricks of Satan (1 John 2:14-16).
B. Listening to worldly wisdom rather than to God's wisdom (Jas. 3:13-18, Prov. 8:1-36).
C. Wallowing in sin (1 John 2:1-6, Prov. 28:13-14).
D. Ignoring the sin issues of their own heart (Jer. 17:9, Mark 7:14-23, Matt. 23:23-26).

IX. The process to evaluate change

A. Examine our own thinking patterns and the things that motivate us to live, to work, to serve, etc. (Rom. 8:5-8, Matt. 6:21-24).
B. Take notice of what we discuss consistently (Luke 6:45).
C. Examine our behavior, attitudes, lifestyle; evaluate things such as how we spend our time, what we produce in life, what we are trying to accomplish in life, the company we keep (Gal. 5:19-22, 6:7-10, 2 Tim. 2:19, 2 Peter 1:1-10, Eph. 5:8-17, Luke 6:43-49, 1 Cor. 15:33, Ps. 1:1-3, 1 Tim. 6:6-12, Matt. 6:19-34).
D. Take notice of how we relate to people (1 John 1:5-2:11, Prov. 27:5-6).

SECTION 6

Progressive Sanctification

I. The definition of <u>sanctification</u>

A. Sanctification is the same Greek word as holiness: *hagios*, meaning a separation ("What Is Sanctification," 2009).

B. Sanctification consists in the removal of the "penal consequences of sin from the moral nature and the progressive implanting and growth of a new principle of life" (Strong, 1886, 869).

C. It is not just "deliverance from sin but development of a life that reflects the very character of God" (Hodge, 1983, 343).

D. It is the "carrying on to perfection the work begun in regeneration, which extends to the whole man" (Easton, 1996).

E. The separation from evil unto God, in position, condition, and life into the very likeness of Jesus Christ.

II. Sanctification divided into three categories

A. Sanctification is a "once-for-all" positional separation into Christ at our salvation (Easton, 1996).

B. Sanctification is a "practical progressive holiness" in a believer's life while awaiting the return of Christ.

C. Sanctification is "the end result of being changed into the perfect likeness of Jesus Christ, set apart in character, and completely separated from the presence of evil" (Easton, 1996).

III. The work of sanctification

A. Sanctification is a work of God.

B. God the Father carries out the work of sanctification through the Holy Spirit who indwells Christians (Strong, 1886, 871).

C. Even though sanctification is a work of God, He invites Christians to be involved in the process (Phil. 2:12-13).

D. Christians are to be devoted to putting off sinful patterns of living in thoughts, desires, words, and actions, while walking in holiness through the power of God (1 John 3:1-3, Eph. 4:17-24).
E. As God works, Christians are to respond by working out in practice what He is doing in them, for them, and through them (Phil. 2:12-13).
F. Christians are working from their new position in Christ in contradiction to their old position under Adam in sin; God has set Christians apart to Himself and empowered them to participate with Him in the process of making Christians like Him in character (Rom. 5:1-6:22).

IV. The Word of God on sanctification

A. In First Corinthians 6:11, the Apostle Paul emphasized the position of sanctification. He used words such as *washed*, *sanctified*, and *justified*. These words were used to emphasize different sides of the reality of being set apart for God (Hodge, 1974, 63).
B. In First John 3:1-3, John communicated to the Christians that they were children of God. These Christians were called to accept the fact that their name set them apart from the godless system of the world.
C. In First Timothy 4:7-10, Paul challenged Timothy to stay away from false teaching and pursue godliness, anticipating the fullness of salvation to come.
D. In Philippians 2:12-13, Paul encouraged the Philippians to be God-pleasers instead of man-pleasers (Lightfoot, 1896). The saints could obey without the presence of Paul because it was God at work within them. God was energizing the saints with their desire and ability to obey (Wuest, 1997).
E. In Ephesians 4:17-24, Paul challenged those Christians to live their lives according to their new position in Jesus Christ. They were challenged to no longer live the way they lived before they were placed in Jesus Christ. What they were in position in Christ was to be reflected in how they lived in practice.
F. In Colossians 3:1-17, Paul explained in detail the purpose and practice of progressive sanctification. He reasoned with Christians to put off particular sinful patterns as a result of their position in Christ, their prize in Christ, and the Person of Christ. In addition, Paul reasoned with them to put off particular sinful patterns and walk in their new character in Christ, knowing they were being transformed into the image of Jesus Christ as result. He also reasoned with them to put on attitudes and actions that reflect the character of Christ, which resulted in their being chosen, made holy, and being the object of God's affections.

V. The sanctification process challenged by the devil

A. Satan is trying to short-circuit the sanctification process through:

1. The *world*—a system and order of life that denies God and His ways and operates according to human nature and demonic influences (Eph. 2:1-4, 1 John 2:15-17, Jas. 3:14-16).
2. *False religion*—organizations and churches that deny that salvation is through Jesus Christ (1 Tim. 4:1, John 14:6, 1 John 4:1-3).
3. *Temptation*—enticing people away from God through the eyes, flesh, and mind (Gen. 3:1-24, Jas. 1:12-15).
4. *Accusations*—condemning Christians by describing their sins to God (Rev. 12:10).
5. *Fear*—trying to make people afraid to share, defend, and live the truth (1 Peter 5:6-10, 1 John 4:4, 2 Tim. 1:6-10).

B. Satan is working through several devices such as:

1. *Deception*—leads people into error about God, life, self, relationships, government, life issues through man-centered philosophies and logical sounding arguments, based on the principles of this world's systems and human traditions promoted through demonic influence and doctrines of demons (2 Cor. 11:3, 14-15, 4:4).
2. Division—seeks to separate people so that they will not work together in ways that promote God's Kingdom; He draws people into selfish ambition, envy, and strife, leading to disorder and every evil thing (Jas. 3:13-16).
3. *Doubt*—seeks to get people to question the validity of God's truth through various philosophies and logical-sounding arguments promoted through demonic influence and doctrines of demons (Gen. 3:1-7).
4. *Desires*—appeals to our desires for food, comfort, sex, significance, satisfaction, security, etc., to lead us into self-centeredness and disobedience to God in those areas; appeals to our corrupted nature to lead us to live for self and to live our own way, resulting in being independent of God and His governing authorities; seeks to provide access to the things we treasure above God and His will so that we will sin to get them and sin when we don't get them (Matt. 4:1-11, Jas. 1:13-17, Gal. 5:19-23).
5. *Distraction*—seeks to keep us preoccupied with matters that are not as important as single-minded devotion to God; gets us focused on human agendas instead of God's agenda (Matt. 16:21-23).

6. *Discouragement*—seeks to get Christians to lose hope in God and His will (1 Peter 5:6-11).
7. *Death*—keeps people in slavery to him through the fear of death since he has power to murder (John 8:44, Heb. 2:14-15).
8. *Disbelief*—seeks to lead people to ignore, deny, disbelieve, distrust, and resist the truth about God, the Bible, themselves, the purpose of life, the reality of death, and many other issues through various man-centered philosophies and logical-sounding arguments promoted through demonic influence and doctrines or demons; this leads to sinful choices and lifestyles that impact others in detrimental ways (Gen. 3:1-11).
9. *Dilution*—seeks to lead Christians to blend in with the world's system by adopting their values, motives, and trends to the point that they have diluted their holiness with worldliness; this leads to lessening the power of their witness for Christ (Jas. 4:4-7, 1 John 2:15-17, 5:19).
10. *Derailment*—seeks to hinder people's progress toward spiritual maturity and discipleship of others through various delays or disruptions in their lives (Rom. 1:13, Rev. 2:10-11).

SECTION 7

Getting to Heart Issues

The Three Basic Responses to *People* and *Circumstances*

People

and

Circumstances

There are three basic responses to people and circumstances

Neutral Responses

Demonstrating and expressing happiness, sadness, disappointment, embarrassment, or hurt that does not violate Scripture; the normal expressions in life that God does not hold against you as wrong.

Loving Responses

to have thoughts, motives, desires, communication patterns, behavior patterns, manner of life patterns, relationship patterns, or serving patterns we are commanded and empowered by God to have that demonstrate love for God and others.

Unloving Responses

to have unloving thoughts, motives, desires, communication patterns, behavior patterns, manner of life patterns, relationship patterns, or serving patterns that are prohibited by God and are determined by the evil in our hearts.

Four Key Issues Revealed in Our Responses to *People* and *Circumstances*

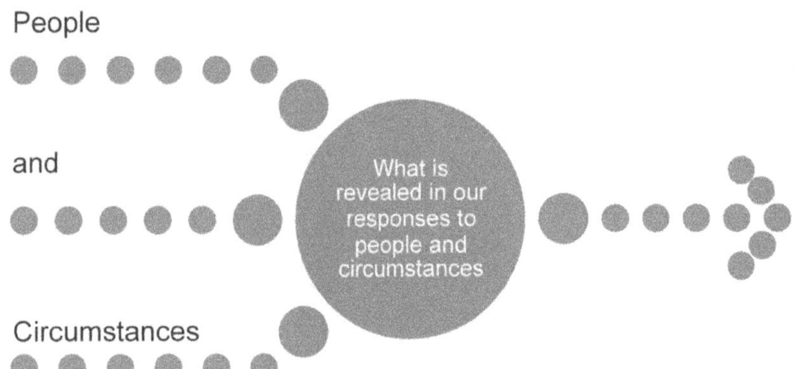

Expectations and desires of life that have become the central focus of our attention above love for God and love for others

Thoughts, motives, desires, communication patterns, behavior patterns, relational patterns, serving patterns that are displeasing to God and that God wants changed for His glory, the good of others, and our good

Thoughts, motives, desires, communication patterns, behavior patterns, relational patterns, serving patterns that are pleasing to God and are glorifying God, good to others, and for our own good

The reality that one does not have a genuine relationship with God and is in need of deliverance from the penalty and power of sin for a new and right relationship with God

What I *Cannot* and *Can* Control

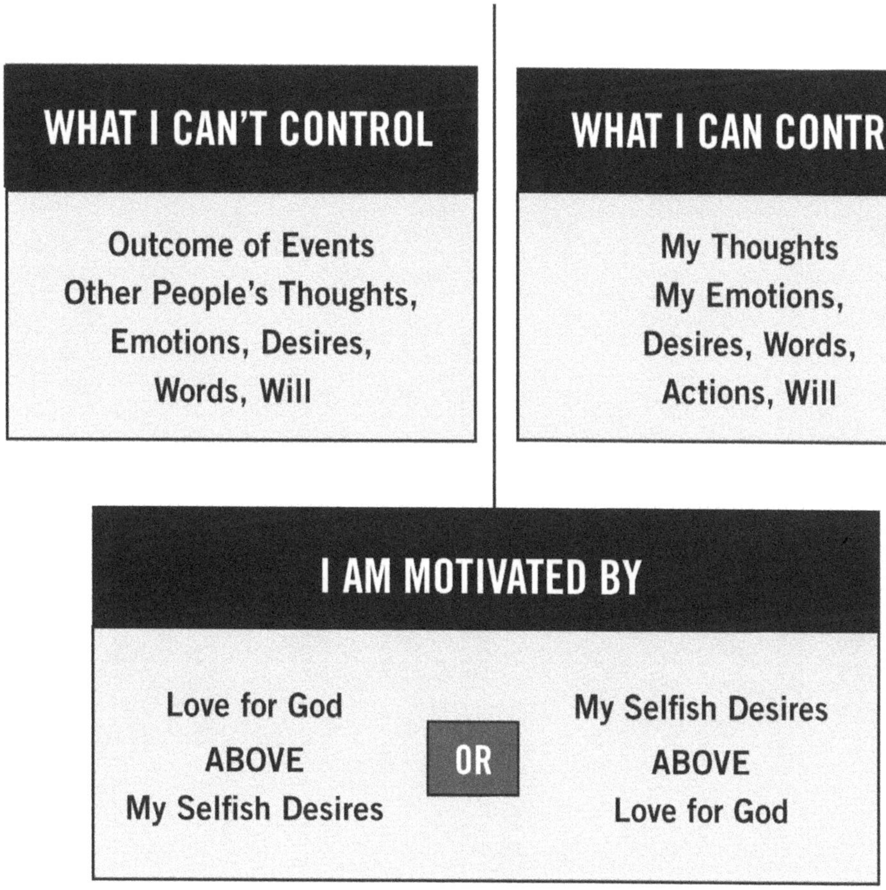

WHAT I CAN'T CONTROL	WHAT I CAN CONTROL
Outcome of Events Other People's Thoughts, Emotions, Desires, Words, Will	My Thoughts My Emotions, Desires, Words, Actions, Will

I AM MOTIVATED BY		
Love for God ABOVE My Selfish Desires	OR	My Selfish Desires ABOVE Love for God

We cannot control people or the outcome of situations (Eccl. 3:1-11, 7:13-14, 9:1-2). We can only control our own thoughts, emotions, desires, words, and actions (Rom. 12:2-3, Prov. 16:32, Ps. 37:4, Eph. 4:29, 22-24). Therefore, we need to evaluate and take responsibility for how we are responding to people and the outcome of situations (Gal. 6:7-8, 5:16-25). We need to evaluate what is motivating us with people and the outcome of situations (Jas. 1:13-14, 3:13-16, 4:1-3). Are we motivated by love for God above our selfish desires? Or, are we motivated by our selfish desires above love for God? (1 John 2:15-16, Jas. 4:4, 3:16).

Looking at Some Central *Heart Issues*

Pride
- Mind set on self; self-centeredness
- Life revolves around what is important to us above what is important to God. When what God says contradicts what we think, we allow what we think to be the perspective we hold above what God says. Interpret the Scripture to fit our agenda.

Lust
- Consumed with what we treasure above loving God and loving others. Willing to sin to get this treasure and to sin when we cannot receive this treasure. This treasure in essence has become an all-consuming desire that we allow to become the center of our attention above loving God and loving others

Idolatry
- Will use people, places, products, or perspectives as means to obtain or to satisfy the lust of our life. They are placed above God to satisfy the lustful desires we treasure above loving God and loving others. They are the means to our lustful end.

Worry
disturbing or disquieting thoughts of the mind as we are consumed with the possibility of losing or not receiving something we treasure

Anger
to have ungodly attitudes, words, or actions as a result of some perceived need, desire, personal preference, or standard not being met by someone or in circumstances

Depression
enslaving thought, mood, or feeling of unhappiness that becomes the reason we give for not functioning as we should

As you walk in pride, you will be consumed with lust. As you are consumed with lust, you will seek idols to satisfy your lustful desires. When the idols seemingly are not going to follow through with your expectation to satisfy your lustful desires, you may begin to worry. When the idols do not follow through on your expectation to satisfy your lustful desires, you may fall into anger. All of this worry and anger could possibly lead you to depression.

As you listen and talk with people, evaluate how you are responding to other people and circumstances. Listen to the dominant topics of conversation to determine what you tend to treasure, dislike, worry about, get angry about. Learn the people, places, products, and perspectives you tend to discuss the most and why. Listen to see if your primary conversations are driven by discussions of yourself or other things more important than yourself. Identify who or what tends to lead you to react in happiness or sadness.

The Development and the Demise of *Lustful Desires* of the *Heart*

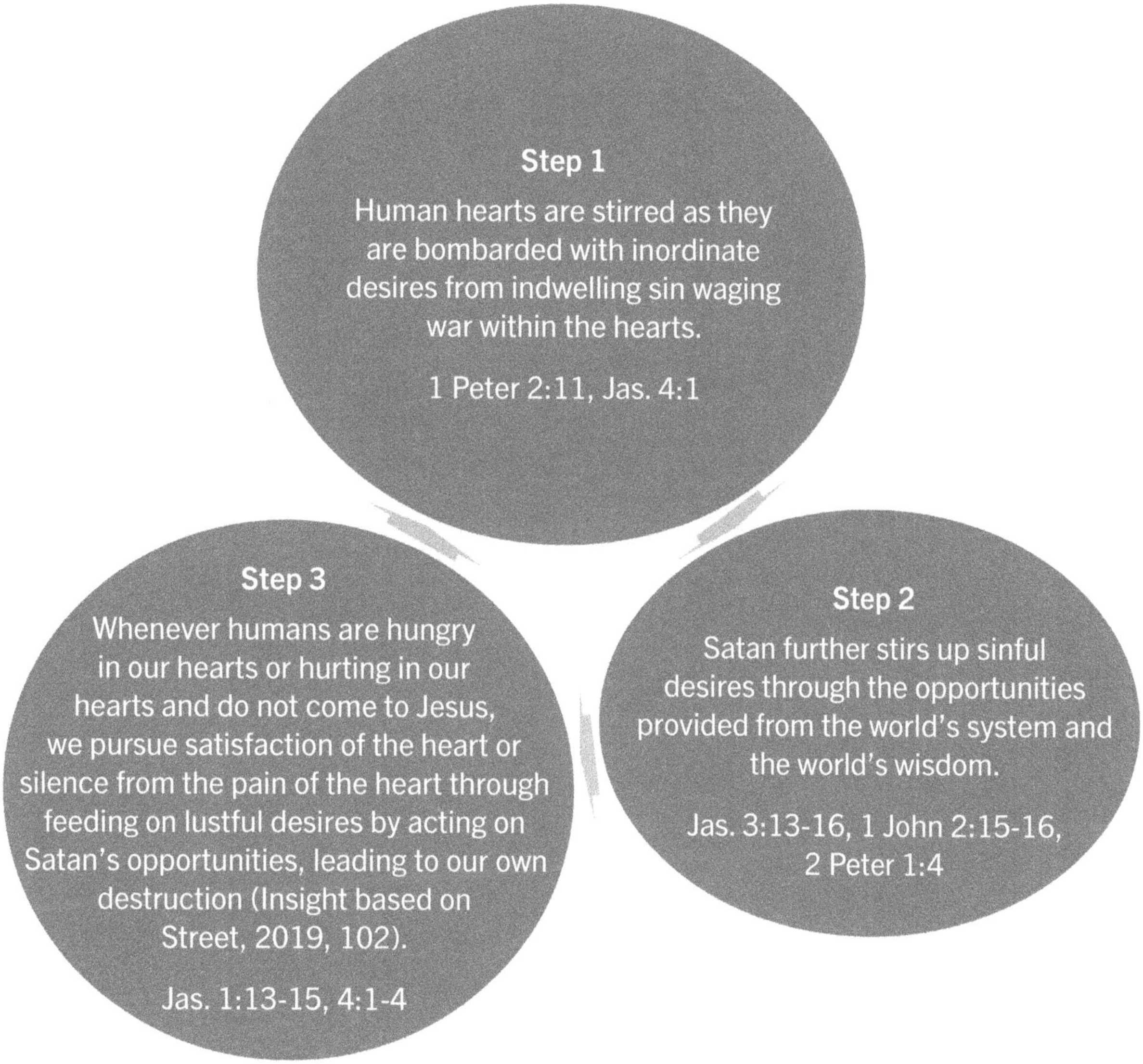

Step 1

Human hearts are stirred as they are bombarded with inordinate desires from indwelling sin waging war within the hearts.

1 Peter 2:11, Jas. 4:1

Step 2

Satan further stirs up sinful desires through the opportunities provided from the world's system and the world's wisdom.

Jas. 3:13-16, 1 John 2:15-16, 2 Peter 1:4

Step 3

Whenever humans are hungry in our hearts or hurting in our hearts and do not come to Jesus, we pursue satisfaction of the heart or silence from the pain of the heart through feeding on lustful desires by acting on Satan's opportunities, leading to our own destruction (Insight based on Street, 2019, 102).

Jas. 1:13-15, 4:1-4

Direction and ***Result*** of Addressing Some Central Heart Issues

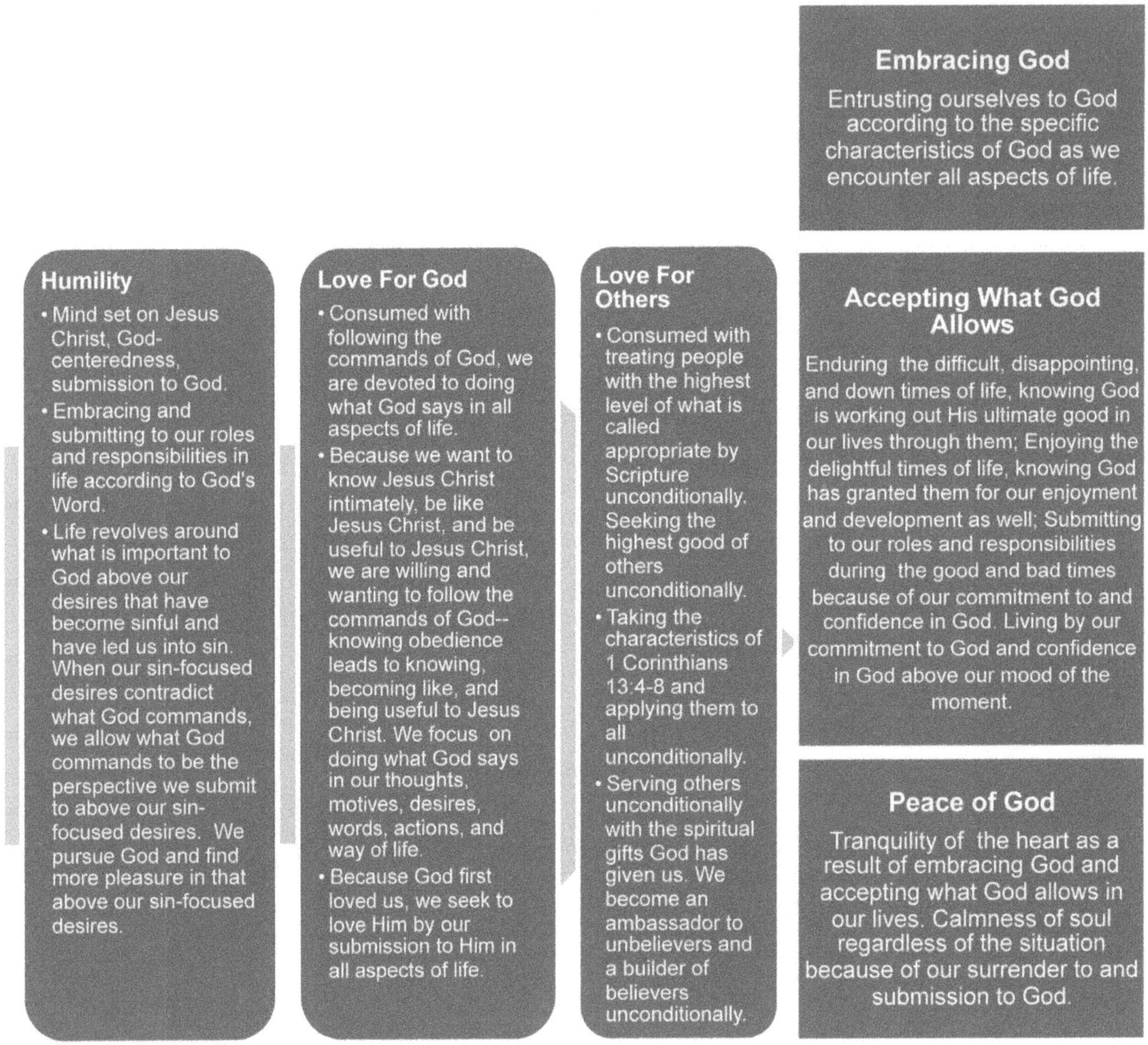

Humility

- Mind set on Jesus Christ, God-centeredness, submission to God.
- Embracing and submitting to our roles and responsibilities in life according to God's Word.
- Life revolves around what is important to God above our desires that have become sinful and have led us into sin. When our sin-focused desires contradict what God commands, we allow what God commands to be the perspective we submit to above our sin-focused desires. We pursue God and find more pleasure in that above our sin-focused desires.

Love For God

- Consumed with following the commands of God, we are devoted to doing what God says in all aspects of life.
- Because we want to know Jesus Christ intimately, be like Jesus Christ, and be useful to Jesus Christ, we are willing and wanting to follow the commands of God--knowing obedience leads to knowing, becoming like, and being useful to Jesus Christ. We focus on doing what God says in our thoughts, motives, desires, words, actions, and way of life.
- Because God first loved us, we seek to love Him by our submission to Him in all aspects of life.

Love For Others

- Consumed with treating people with the highest level of what is called appropriate by Scripture unconditionally. Seeking the highest good of others unconditionally.
- Taking the characteristics of 1 Corinthians 13:4-8 and applying them to all unconditionally.
- Serving others unconditionally with the spiritual gifts God has given us. We become an ambassador to unbelievers and a builder of believers unconditionally.

Embracing God

Entrusting ourselves to God according to the specific characteristics of God as we encounter all aspects of life.

Accepting What God Allows

Enduring the difficult, disappointing, and down times of life, knowing God is working out His ultimate good in our lives through them; Enjoying the delightful times of life, knowing God has granted them for our enjoyment and development as well; Submitting to our roles and responsibilities during the good and bad times because of our commitment to and confidence in God. Living by our commitment to God and confidence in God above our mood of the moment.

Peace of God

Tranquility of the heart as a result of embracing God and accepting what God allows in our lives. Calmness of soul regardless of the situation because of our surrender to and submission to God.

As you walk in humility, you will be preoccupied with love for God. As you are preoccupied with love for God, you will develop in genuine love for others. As you walk in love for God and love for others, you will develop in embracing God and accepting what God allows as you live by your trust in the Person, plans, precepts, and promises of God. Living this way involves living by your commitment to God and confidence in God above your mood of the moment. As you develop in living by your commitment to God and confidence in God, you will experience the peace of God in your life on a consistent basis in the good and bad of life.

Overall, as you develop in living by humility, love for God and others, embracing God, and accepting what God allows, you will not only experience the peace of God consistently, but you will find yourself turning away from a life reduced to making God, people, and circumstances the help to or the complaint against your accomplishing your personal ambitions. Living a life where you make God, people, and circumstances the help to or the complaint against your accomplishing your personal ambitions reveals your pride, lust, idolatry, worry, or anger, which can lead to depression in your life.

Evaluate your life and see where you stand. Identify where you are lacking in humility, in love for God and others, in embracing God, in accepting what God allows, and in the peace of God. Move into the process of remorse over your sin, renouncing of your sin, repenting of your sin, renewing your mind in the truth of humility, love for God and others, embracing God, accepting what God allows, and the peace of God. Replace the pride, lust, idolatry, worry, anger (and all other sins discovered), which can lead to depression—with humility, love for God and others, embracing God, and accepting what God allows, which will result in the peace of God on a consistent basis in the good and bad of life.

You will see a difference in your life when you start living for God and stop living for yourself. People and circumstances will be handled by God's agenda. You will find that life is more satisfying and productive as you live to please God instead of seeking to use God, people, or circumstances to accomplish what is and has been more important to you above your allegiance to and obedience to God. You will find that life is more satisfying and productive as you live to please God, instead of being worried or angry with God, people, or circumstances as a result of their falling short of providing what is and has been more important to you above your allegiance to and obedience to God.

SECTION 8

Establishing Involvement with Counselees

Man-Centered Involvement	**God-Centered Involvement**
Helps people to identify and change their mistaken beliefs about self, others, and life, and to participate more fully in a social world.	Helps people identify and change sinful beliefs about self, others, life, and God; Helps them participate in genuine fellowship with God and other Christians as they interact in the world without functioning according to the world's system but by the Word of God (2 Cor. 10:3-5).
Helps people to disclose and reevaluate feelings and behavior patterns, to understand and accept previously rejected aspects of themselves, to take risks, to become more open and honest about themselves, to learn new methods of living with self and others, and to gain new satisfactions from life.	Helps people to disclose and reevaluate feelings and behavior in light of God's Word in order to learn who they are and who they are not according to God's Word. This leads them to put off sinful methods of living and to live by righteousness gained by faith in the Person and work of Jesus Christ; This results in living for God and enjoying satisfaction gained from living for God (Rom. 12:1-3, Eph. 4:1-32, John 15:1-11).
Focuses on self-efficacy—the person's belief or expectation that he or she can master a situation and bring about desired change.	Focuses on self-sacrifice—denying self, taking up his or her cross and following Jesus Christ. The person has the belief that through the power of God, he/she can be and do all that God commands (Matt. 16:24-26, Phil. 2:12-13).
Takes stock in choosing a direction that best suits a person.	Takes stock in leading a person into choosing God's will in all aspects of life (Col. 1:28-29).

Man-Centered Involvement	God-Centered Involvement
Has the belief system that individuals are the authors of their lives and can design the pathways they want to follow.	Has the belief system that people are created in the image of God and are created for His glory and should therefore submit to God's will and way for their existence (Gen. 1:26-27, Is. 43:7, Col. 1:13-29).
Focuses on significant personality change and adjustment to situational and life problems.	Focuses on transformation of character into the image of Christ in all aspects of life so that individuals may function to the glory of God and have stability that comes from operating according to the glory of God in life situations (2 Cor. 3:17-4:18, Col. 3:1-25).

Ten-Point Summary of 1 John 4:7-21

I. We are commanded to love one another, which is ultimately seeking the highest good of others in any or all aspects of life without looking for anything in return for our service toward them.

II. The source of this quality of love we are commanded to give to one another is from God, Who is by nature and action the epitome of love.

III. The demonstration of this quality of love is seen in God the Father in sending God the Son:

A. to be crucified on the cross, buried, and resurrected on our behalf
B. to deliver us from the penalty of sin, the power of sin, and soon the presence of sin, into a new life in union with Christ Jesus, for those of us who put our faith in the Person and work of Jesus Christ.

IV. God loved us in this fashion because this was His nature, not because we loved Him.

V. We are to love others because of the reality that God loved us first.

VI. We are to love others according to who we are in Christ and the power we have in Christ, not according to who people are or how they treat us or mistreat us.

VII. Since we have the Holy Spirit indwelling us, we have the power to love people according to the ability granted to us by the Holy Spirit, which is not contingent upon the attitudes and actions of others.

VIII. Even though no one has seen God, the evidence that we

A. have embraced the love of God for us,
B. have embraced Jesus as the Son of God,
C. possess a real relationship with God and are not just professing a relationship with God,
D. will be confirmed by the Holy Spirit within us and demonstrated by our obedience to God, leading us to love others with the quality of love that God demonstrated to us.

IX. The more we embrace the love of God for us, pursue walking in obedience to God in all aspects of life, and demonstrate God's quality of love to others:

A. we will grow to maturity in Christ-like character.
B. we will have confidence before God in the day of judgment, because we have walked in love for God and others and reflected His character of love in this world.
C. we will not be fearful of punishment from God.

X. Genuine love for God will always result in genuine love for others, not hatred, or that person does not know and love God at all. Do you love God or do you love him not?

Summary: God designed relationships to revolve around truth and love as demonstrated by God through the community of the Trinity and to be developed through humans' relationship with God and with others. "Man is a social being. He is made to be in relationship with others. This is part of being created in the image of God. The Bible teaches that the one God exists in three persons, Father, Son, and Holy Spirit, who live together in eternal fellowship. So too we were made to live in communion with others. But in particular we were made to live in fellowship and communion with God himself" (Barcley, 2010, 126). This communion with God and others is based on truth and love.

How Do We Develop Involvement in a Loving Manner?

I. Bear with one another (Col. 3:13)—to put up with; to endure; to show self-restraint toward the unpleasantness of others and/or the non-sinful but annoying habits of others.

"bearing with one another, and forgiving each other, whoever has a complaint against anyone; just as the Lord forgave you, so also should you."

II. Be kind to one another (Eph. 4:32)—be useful; be good to others.

"Be kind to one another, tender-hearted, forgiving each other, just as God in Christ also has forgiven you."

III. Comfort one another (1 Thess. 4:18)—to come alongside in order to console, to cheer up, to provide support.

"Therefore comfort one another with these words."

IV. Speak truthfully to one another (Eph. 4:25)—to provide the facts; to maintain integrity with others by being honest in sharing that which is right and real in the sight of God appropriately.

"Therefore, laying aside falsehood, speak truth each one of you with his neighbor, for we are members of one another."

V. Admonish one another (Rom. 15:14)—to teach on proper behavior and belief; to rebuke for wrongdoing; to warn about the consequences of wrong behavior.

"And concerning you, my brethren, I myself also am convinced that you yourselves are full of goodness, filled with all knowledge and able also to admonish one another."

VI. Stimulate one another to love and good deeds (Heb. 10:24)—to stir up by strong argument to seek the highest good of others, along with acts that will be beneficial to others according to God's will and way.

"and let us consider how to stimulate one another to love and good deeds"

VII. Seek good for one another (1 Thess. 5:15)—to be useful, beneficial, profitable according to what is morally right in the sight of God.

"See that no one repays another with evil for evil, but always seek after that which is good for one another and for all people."

What Are the Implications for Building Involvement with the Opposite Sex?

I. Every man or woman is to be loved in such a way that he or she would encounter the love of God through you as you treat the person as you would want to be treated and even better than you would want to be treated, as we relate as ambassadors for Jesus Christ and builders of His Kingdom people.

II. Every man or woman is to be loved in such a way that he or she would encounter the love of God through you as you treat the person as you would a brother, sister, mother, or father, as we relate as ambassadors for Jesus Christ and builders of His kingdom people.

III. Every man or woman is to be loved in such a way that he or she would encounter the love of God through you as you correct them as you would a brother, sister, mother, or father, as we relate as ambassadors for Jesus Christ and builders of His Kingdom people.

IV. Treating the opposite sex as a brother, sister, mother, or father as you respectfully and lovingly correct would promote holiness and God-honoring love between the opposite sexes, as we relate as ambassadors for Jesus Christ and builders of His Kingdom people.

V. Treating the opposite sex as a brother, sister, mother, or father as you respectfully and lovingly correct would help men and women function as God-honoring family members to one another, as opposed to illegitimate lovers with one another, thereby promoting a community of relating that God intended before the Fall of Adam and Eve, as we relate as ambassadors for Jesus Christ and builders of His Kingdom people.

What About Confidentiality and Gaining Involvement through Counseling?

I. Absolute confidentiality is not scriptural. In certain circumstances the Bible requires that facts be disclosed to select others (Matt. 18:15-17).

II. There are certain situations in which information about individuals undergoing counseling may be released with or without their permission. These situations are as follows (Rom. 13:1-3):

A. Where it is proven that children are physically abused, neglected, or sexually abused.
B. In emergency situations where it is proven that there may be danger to the counselee or others; as with homicide or suicide, confidentiality may be broken.
C. If a court of law issues a legitimate subpoena relating to a child abuse case, counselors are required by law to provide the information specifically described in the subpoena;
D. If an unreported life-threatening felony has been committed, counselors are required by law to report it to the police.

III. Counselors may also consult with others or appropriate church ministry staff members regarding certain matters. This could involve issues such as:

A. Church discipline matters
B. Seeking wise counsel to help address the matter in a thorough manner
C. Reporting to other leaders on the status of counseling when feasible and appropriate
D. Training of other counselors to learn how to handle cases of the same nature

SECTION 9

Gathering Data

In order to help people with their problems, we must first gather the proper information so we can have a proper understanding to serve accordingly.

I. Provide an intake form that will collect basic information, i.e., name, birth date, address, marital status, etc.

II. Identify the various dynamics of the family relationship, i.e., past, present, future, tragic events, delightful events, difficult times, relationship with siblings, relationship with parents, etc.

III. Identify the nature of the person's salvation status.

IV. Identify the important issues or events the person believes has shaped and influenced his or her life.

V. Identify this person's understanding of God, self, people, and life circumstances. Learn what events, circumstances, or people have been a shaping influence to the person's understanding of God, self, people, and life circumstances.

VI. Ask questions that help you clarify the facts that have been presented or facts you are unsure about.

VII. Ask questions that help draw out what a person is thinking, feeling, wanting, doing, should be doing, or should not be doing.

VIII. Find out what is happening or has happened to the person in relation to the reason they have come for counseling.

IX. As you identify what is happening or has happened to the person, identify what the person could control within the circumstances, i.e., his or her own thoughts, desires, intentions, emotions, words, or actions.

X. As you identify what is happening or has happened to the person, identify what the person cannot control within the circumstances, i.e., the thoughts, desires, intentions, emotions, words, or will of another person.

XI. Find out what the person's perceptions, preferences, pains, passions are in connection to what is happening or has happened in relation to people and circumstances.

XII. Identify how the person is responding in thoughts, desires, intentions, emotions, words, or actions in relation to what is happening or has happened and connected to other people and circumstances, i.e., neutral, loving, and unloving responses and choices.

XIII. Identify the time frame of responses the person has/had in relation to people and circumstances, i.e., neutral, loving, and unloving responses and choices.

XIV. Find out what the person wants that he/she cannot control getting and what he/she is getting that he/she does not want and cannot control getting in relation to people and circumstances.

XV. Identify what resources are needed to address this problem.

XVI. Identify if other people are required to address this problem.

XVII. Find out who is responsible for which areas of the issue in order to address the problem accordingly.

XVIII. Find out if this is a problem requiring a person to do what they are humanly responsible to do as designed by God.

XIX. Find out if this is a problem requiring family members to do what they are humanly responsible to do as designed by God.

XX. Identify if this is a problem requiring a God-allowed business or institution to do what they are morally responsible to do according to the standards of God.

XXI. Identify if this is a problem requiring governmental institutions to do what they are responsible to do as ordered by God.

XXII. Identify if this is a problem requiring God-given churches to do what they are responsible to do as ordered by God.

XXIII. Identify if this is a problem requiring divine intervention.

Big Picture for Biblical Counseling

I. There are only two central commands that sum up all commands:

A. Love God
B. Love others

II. Man's basic problem is a lack of love of God or a lack of love of others, which is what sin is: As Jesus said, "If you love Me you will keep My commandments / Love your neighbor as yourself." To disobey God is to sin. To sin is to lack love for God and to lack love for others.

III. Man's lack of love for God and others shows up in five places:

A. Category 1 (C1). Thoughts, motives, desires
B. Category 2 (C2). Communicating
C. Category 3 (C3). Behavior / manner of life / conduct / commitments
D. Category 4 (C4). Relating to others
E. Category 5 (C5). Serving others

IV. We will see a lack of love for God or others in areas C1 through C5 as we observe people's actions, reactions, or responses to other people and circumstances.

V. Our mission is to help people see the lack of love for God or others in areas C1-C5 and to help them move from a lack of love for God and others to walking in love for God and others.

VI. The root lack of love will be found in C1.

VII. The fruit lack of love will be found in C2-C5.

VIII. We will help people understand how C1 is driving C2-C5.

IX. We will then lead them to walk in love for God and others in C1-C5.

X. The tools we have to do this are the counseling worksheets and assigned homework.

XI. Therefore as we observe people's actions, reactions, or responses to other people and circumstances or listen to them talk about these issues, we should listen, identify, and document our observations on seven basic levels:

A. Level 1. Listen, identify, and document the C1-C5 issues being presented or discussed.
B. Level 2. Listen, identify, and document what they can and cannot control according to the issues presented or discussed.
C. Level 3. Listen, identify, and document the person's actions, reactions, or responses to other people and circumstances being presented or discussed.
D. Level 4. Listen, identify, and document where their actions, reactions, or responses fit on the biblical framework.
E. Level 5. Listen, identify, and document the belief systems, agendas, and desires being revealed from their actions, reactions, or responses being presented or discussed.
F. Level 6. Listen, identify, and document the pride, lust, and idols being revealed from their actions, reactions, or responses being presented or discussed.
G. Level 7. Listen, identify, and document the C2-C5 issues that are the by-products of the C1 issues.

XII. We will lead them to see and understand these things through the worksheets and homework we will give them.

XIII. We will lead them to renounce, repent, and replace these things with love for God and love for others through the worksheets and homework we will give them.

XIV. We will lead them to do all of this according to the phases and stages of change the person is in.

SECTION 10

Discerning Problems Biblically

In seeking to discern the problems biblically, we must think through key questions.

I. What has gone wrong?

II. What was the cause of this problem?

III. Who was the cause of this problem?

IV. Is this the natural order of consequences for something that should not exist?

V. Is this the natural order of consequences for something that is functioning outside of God's designed order for its existence?

VI. What significant thoughts are revealed by the counselee in the session (in other words, what the counselee presents as the issue(s) and her/his interpretation of those issues)?

VII. In what significant areas of life do these issues exist?

A. Area 1. Thoughts, belief systems, intentions, agendas, motives, desires, emotions
B. Area 2. Communication patterns
C. Area 3. Behavior / manner of life patterns
D. Area 4. Relational patterns
E. Area 5. Serving patterns

VIII. What are the category or categories of issues presented by the counselee?

A. Suffering issue—distress or pain experienced within his/her control or outside his/her control.
B. Salvation issue—unbeliever in need of putting faith in the Person and work of Jesus Christ.
C. Sin/Sanctification issue—believer missing the mark in some area of life and in need of guidance in the process of realization, remorse, renouncing, repenting, renewing, and replacing.
D. Soma issue—physiological issues that are caused by spiritual matters, or physiological issues that just physiological in nature.
E. Sage issue—issues of wisdom requiring practical guidance.

IX. What could he/she control in light of issue(s) presented?

X. What could he/she not control in light of issue(s) presented?

XI. How did he/she respond, react, or make choices in light of the issue(s) presented?

A. Neutral—responses such disappointment, grief, sadness, or happiness, as those are not considered as right or wrong in the sight of God.
B. Loving—thoughts, desires, words, or actions that are right and godly in the sight of God.
C. Unloving—thoughts, desires, words, or actions that are wrong and ungodly in the sight of God.

XII. What heart issues are being revealed about the counselee in light of the issue(s) presented?

A. Prideful Belief Systems—being self-centered.
B. Motives/Agendas/Intentions—goals centered around getting one's way.
C. Emotions—being demonstrated and what are they revealing
D. Lust—They want______ at the level of sinning to get it and sinning if they don't get it
E. Idol—They are using this person, place, product, perspective, platform, power, or position in ways that are evil and selfish to gain this lustful desire.
F. Anger—They have the mindset or manner that is ungodly and antagonistic; they are having a temper tantrum because they are not able to have what they want or getting what they don't want.

G. Worry—They are consumed with ungodly fear of not getting what they want, losing what they have, or receiving something they don't want, instead of trusting God and accepting what He allows.

H. Any other heart issues

XIII. What phase is the counselee in with problem(s) presented by the counselee and significant thoughts revealed by him/her in session (Circle which one applies)?

A. *Not yet in any phase*—There is no realization, remorse, renouncing, repenting, renewing, or replacing in light of the issues presented.

B. *Realization Phase*—He/she has a biblical understanding of God's Word in light of the issues presented.

C. *Remorse Phase*—He/she has a biblical understanding of God's Word in light of the issues presented, sees his/her sin condition in light of the issues presented, and has godly sorrow in light of the issues presented.

D. *Renounce Phase*—He/she has a biblical understanding of God's Word in light of the issues presented, sees his/her sin condition in light of the issues presented, has godly sorrow in light of the issues presented, and is confessing his/her sin accordingly.

E. *Repent Phase*—He/she has a biblical understanding of God's Word in light of the issues presented, sees his/her sin condition in light of the issues presented, has godly sorrow in light of the issues presented, is confessing his/her sin, and is turning away from the sin accordingly.

F. *Renew Phase*—He/she has a biblical understanding of God's Word in light of the issues presented, sees his/her sin condition in light of the issues presented, has godly sorrow in light of the issues presented, is confessing his/her sin, is turning away from the sin accordingly, and is learning and meditating on the Scriptures that guide him/her into the godly way of living in light of the issues presented.

G. *Replace Phase*—He/she has a biblical understanding of God's Word in light of the issues presented, sees his/her sin condition in light of the issues presented, has godly sorrow in light of the issues presented, is confessing his/her sin, is turning away from the sin accordingly, is learning and meditating on the Scriptures that guide him/her into the godly way of living in light of the issues presented, and is putting to practice the godly way of living in light of the issues presented.

XIV. **What biblical principles need to be discussed in light of the issues presented and the phase the counselee is in, according to the issues presented?**

XV. **What application assignments need to be given in light of the issues presented and the phase the counselee is in, according to the issues presented?**

XVI. **How is God glorified in the resolution of this problem?**

XVII. **How are individuals moved to function according to a God-given order through discussion and resolution of this problem?**

XVIII. **How are families moved to function according to a God-given order through discussion and resolution of this problem?**

XIX. **How are God-led churches moved to function according to their God-given order through discussion and resolution of this problem?**

XX. **How can humanity consider embracing salvation or sanctification through discussion and resolution of this problem?**

SECTION 11

Providing Instruction

As we seek to give instruction in counseling, let us consider these particular factors below.

I. **Directive instruction before the Fall—Before the Fall, God provided directive instruction—guidance for what humanity was to do in creation (Gen. 1:26–2:25).**

II. **Corrective instruction after the Fall—After the Fall, corrective instruction became necessary, challenging humanity's sinful actions and giving direction for what must now be done in light of the sinful condition of mankind (Gen. 3:9–24).**

III. **The Person of the Holy Spirit—The Holy Spirit is not merely a force or an influence, but the third Person of the Trinity—Father, Son, and Holy Spirit. He is equal in nature and character to God the Father and God the Son.** The Spirit possesses the divine attributes of the Father and the Son and performs the work that only God can accomplish (Matt. 28:19; 2 Cor. 13:14; Acts 5:3–4). He leads us into truth, convicts of sin, points us to our Lord and Savior Jesus Christ, enables us to put to death the deeds of the flesh, and empowers us to walk in holiness.

IV. **The Spirit's role in instruction—The ministry of the Holy Spirit is essential for providing instruction in the Christian life (John 14:26; 16:12–15; 1 Cor. 2:10–16).**

V. **God's instruction in Scripture—God provides instruction to His people through both the Old and New Testaments:**

A. The Ten Commandments (Ex. 20)
B. The Great Commission (Matt. 28:18-20)
C. The Sermon on the Mount (Matt. 5:1–7:29)

VI. The authority of Scripture—Scripture is the ultimate standard of truth that God uses to provide instruction (John 17:17).

VII. The reliability of Scripture—God's Word does not affirm anything that is contrary to fact (Ps. 19:7–11).

VIII. The command to obey Scripture—We are called to follow the commands of Scripture, whether given explicitly or by implication (1 John 2:3–6; John 14:21).

IX. The warning against compromise—We must not follow or obey any standard or insight that contradicts Scripture (Col. 2:8; Rom. 12:2).

X. Truth aims at love—"The goal of our instruction is love from a pure heart and a good conscience and a sincere faith" (1 Tim. 1:5). As John Piper explains, "Truth aims at love" (Piper, 2014).

XI. Love aims at truth—Love "does not rejoice in unrighteousness, but rejoices with the truth" (1 Cor. 13:6). Thus, love is inseparably bound to truth (Piper, 2014).

XII. Love shapes truth—"Speaking the truth in love, we are to grow up in all aspects into Him who is the head, even Christ" (Eph. 4:15). This means truth must always be spoken with love (Piper, 2014).

XIII. Truth shapes love—"By this we know that we love the children of God, when we love God and observe [follow] His commandments. For this is the love of God, that we keep His commandments; and His commandments are not burdensome" (1 John 5:2–3). In this way, love is defined and governed by truth (Piper, 2014).

XIV. **Contrast with humanistic counseling—This biblical understanding of instruction stands in sharp contrast to the humanistic counseling models that orient people toward *their own internal value systems* rather than toward God's revealed truth.** From a secular standpoint, "the counseling task is to assist individuals in finding answers that are most congruent with their own values" (Jones, 2010, introduction). Within this framework, clients are expected to *identify their personal values and goals, make autonomous decisions, and take responsibility for the results* (Corey, 2016, 7-8). Furthermore, counselors are prohibited from imposing any value system; their role is to ensure that clients apply *their own values* in addressing life's challenges (ACA, quoted in Corey, 2016, 14–15). Although this appears respectful on the surface, it ultimately elevates human autonomy above divine authority. Such an approach conflicts with Scripture's insistence that true instruction must flow from *God's Word*, not from the shifting moral compass of the human heart.

XV. **The nature of truth—"Truth is the basis of all true love. It is not simply an intellectual property. It is that which lives in and directs life. Jesus is the truth that creates such love. This truth is eternal and must be guarded carefully (Piper, 2014).**

XVI. **Loving in truth through gospel care—To love in truth is to engage in a biblical, personal ministry that helps others become more like Jesus. As Scott Mehl describes, "Gospel care is the God-exalting, grace-saturated art of patiently knowing, sacrificially serving, truthfully speaking, and consistently applying the gospel in order to help others become more like Jesus" (Mehl, 2020, 35).**

XVII. **Love and truth in fellowship—Love that reflects the character of God is always governed and guided by truth. As Mark Dever notes, Christian fellowship "is created by truth and exhibited in love. Each qualifies the other. Our love grows soft if it is not strengthened by truth, and our truth hard if it is not softened by love" (Dever, 2014). Therefore, the church must hold together both love and truth, avoiding extremes that emphasize one at the expense of the other.**

SECTION 12

Biblical Hope

Definition of Hope: *Expectation of a desired outcome*

I. Hope that comes from God will not *disappoint* us (Rom. 5:1-5).

A. This hope is *provided* by God's grace to us (Rom. 5:1-2).
B. This hope is *produced* through tribulation, perseverance, and developed character (Rom. 5:3-4).
C. This hope is *promoted* by the Holy Spirit (Rom. 5:5).

II. Hope that comes from man's opinions will deceive us (Prov. 16:25).

A. False hope is *built* on human ideas (Prov. 14:12).

1. All my problems would be solved if I had a better job.
2. If I could have who and what I want in life, I would be happy.
3. If my husband/wife would just give me my way, I would be happy and all my problems would be solved.

B. False hope is *based* on an improper interpretation of Scripture (2 Peter 3:14-18).

1. Since God owns it all, I should never be without.
2. Since God is my Father, I should be healed of all diseases.
3. God will give me anything I want if I just ask for it.
4. We should call those things that are not as though they are.

C. False hope is *birthed* by the passions of ungodly men (2 Peter 2:1-3).

1. If I treat people right, I will not be mistreated by others.
2. If I can believe it, then I can achieve it.
3. There is a perfect mate for everyone.
4. If I serve others, surely they will return the favor and serve me.

III. Hope that comes from God will draw us near to God (Heb. 7:11-19).

A. This hope *drives* us to depend on Christ (Heb. 7:11-19).
   1. We can expect God to never leave us or forsake us (Heb. 13:5-6).
   2. We can expect God to be our help in time of need (Heb. 4:14-16).
   3. We can expect God to help us make it through every trial and temptation we face (1 Cor. 10:13).
   4. We can expect God to provide all we need according to His riches in glory in Christ Jesus (Phil. 4:19).

B. This hope *develops* stability in our faith (Heb. 6:13-19).
   1. Because we have been saved, we can expect to live in heaven with Jesus (John 14:1-4).
   2. Because we have been saved, we can expect to receive a glorified body like Jesus Christ (Phil. 3:20-21).
   3. Because we have been saved, we can expect God to perfect the things concerning us (Ps. 138:8).

C. This hope *deepens* our confidence in Christ (Phil. 1:12-21).
   1. We can expect God to work all things together for our good (Rom. 8:28).
   2. We can expect God to do exceedingly abundantly more than all we could ever ask or think (Eph. 3:20).
   3. We can expect God to order our steps (Ps. 37:23).

IV. Hope that comes from God will *direct* us to the return of Christ (1 John 3:1-3).

A. This hope leads us to *focus* on Christ and His glory (Titus 2:11-14).
B. This hope leads us to *favor* the blessings we will receive at His return (1 Peter 1:13).
C. This hope leads us to *forsake* our sin so we can be like Christ (1 John 3:1-3).

V. Hope deferred can be expectations that are delayed or denied (Prov. 13:12).

A. There are things we are hoping for that will not be realized, resulting in deep disappointments in our lives.
B. There are things we are hoping for that will be realized but are on delay according to the providential plans and wisdom of God.

C. The things that God has promised to us in His Word will be realized in our lives, and things God has not promised to us in His Word may or may not be realized in our lives.

VI. Where our expectations are denied, our hearts will be sick, i.e., disappointed. God's not granting those expectations reveals that they were not promised by God nor did those expectations fit in God's providential plan for us. Therefore, it is to our advantage to learn what God has not promised (Prov. 13:12).

A. God never promised freedom from trials and problems.
B. God never promised that everything we do would work out as we planned and practiced.
C. God never promised that everyone would treat us well, even as we treat them well. In essence, God never promised that our faithful input into matters and our God-honoring pursuit of particular desires would produce our expected success and the realization of all we faithfully pursue.

VII. Disappointed expectations can lead us to the end of false hope and into building genuine *faith* in what God has promised as we wait on the fulfillment of those promises that are delayed in realization.

A. Disappointed expectations can lead us to focusing on the <u>*reformation*</u> of our existence in totality to reflect the character of Jesus Christ, which God promised would happen (Phil. 3:20-21, Ps. 138:8).
B. Disappointed expectations can lead us to focusing on the <u>*responsibility*</u> of God to provide, protect, and prepare us for the next life, which God promised would happen (Phil. 1:6, 4:19, Heb. 13:5-6).
C. Disappointed expectations can lead us to focus on the <u>*rewards*</u> of God in this life and the life to come, which God promised would happen (Heb. 11:6, Gal. 6:9, 1 Cor. 3:7-15).
D. Disappointed expectations can lead us to focus on the <u>*return*</u> of Christ and His glory, along with the <u>*residence*</u> created by our Lord and Savior Jesus Christ when He returns for us, which God promised would happen (1 John 3:1-3, John 14:3).

VIII. You must take time to discern the kind of hope that lies within you.

A. <u>*Examine*</u> your life and see what your hope is placed in.
B. <u>*Consider*</u> who or what you are depending on to bring it to pass.
C. <u>*Determine*</u> if what you are hoping for is promised to you by God.

IX. You must take time to develop in the hope that comes from God (Heb. 12:1-3).

A. *Identify* what false hopes you have been trusting in.
B. *Consider* the specific promises of God you need to hope in, as a replacement of the false hopes you have been trusting in.
C. *Replace* those false hopes you have been trusting in with the specific promises of God.

SECTION 13

Guilt and Repentance

2 Corinthians 7:10-11

I. When sorrow over sin functions as God intends, a person will move into the practice of repentance leading to salvation (v10) (Ps. 51:1-4, Matt. 26:69-75, Acts 2:36-41, 1 Thess.1:6-9, Luke 19:8-10).

A. *Definition* of godly sorrow—Godly sorrow can be defined as having grief over sin in regards to God. A person is grieved over the reality that he/she has offended the Almighty God. This person has a sense of guilt with a desire and will to turn away from that which has offended God. Godly sorrow emphasizes the relationship with the Person of God instead of the consequences of the sin. In other words, the person is sorrowful because of offending God, not because of the punishment. This is why we also call it contrite sorrow.

B. *Direction* of godly sorrow—Godly sorrow leads us in the direction of repentance toward God. Repentance is the act of changing one's mind, resulting in a change of action toward sin. It is not merely feeling bad and seeing sin differently. It is seeing sin from God's perspective, resulting in a change of purpose and life away from the sin. This why we call it contrite sorrow.

C. *Destination* of godly sorrow—Godly sorrow leads a person to salvation. Salvation is a deliverance from sin, resulting in a right relationship/fellowship with God and all that comes with the right relationship/fellowship.

II. When sorrow over sin functions according to the world's standard, a person will not repent of his/her sin, resulting in death (v10) (Ex. 9:27-35, Matt. 27:3-5, Gen. 4:1-14).

A. *Definition* of worldly sorrow—Worldly sorrow can be defined as grief over the consequences of sin. It is a grief in connection with the results sin brings. This person has a sense of guilt yet she/he is not willing to turn away from the sin. Sorrow that functions in line with the world mourns the consequences of sin without considering God. A person functioning in worldly sorrow has a fear of what is going to happen to him/her as a result of getting caught. It is remorse over sin with a change of mind about the sin but not change of purpose or life away from the sin.

B. *Direction* of worldly sorrow—Worldly sorrow leads us away from God instead of to God. Those who walk in worldly sorrow focus on relief of pain instead of a relationship with God. Worldly sorrow leads to a preoccupation with self instead of preoccupation with God's redemption.
C. *Destination* of worldly sorrow—Worldly sorrow leads to death. Death is separation from God, resulting in a disconnect from the power, provision, promises, and personal presence of God and all that results from that disconnect. This is why we call it casualty sorrow.

III. There are certain indicators of worldly sorrow (v10) (Gen. 4:1-14, Mark 10:17-22, Ex. 9:27-35, Matt. 27:3-5).

A. Sorrow over what will *happen* to us as a result of our sin but no concern over how our sin has dishonored God or damaged others (Gen. 4:1-14).
B. Sorrow over *sin* in the situation but being unwilling to let go of the treasure that keeps us in sin and away from genuine fellowship with God (Mark 10:17-22).
C. Sorrow over the situation, acknowledgment of sin, and acknowledgment of the character of God, but no *reverence* for God or fear of God's judgment in the matter (Ex. 9:27-35).
D. Sorrow over the situation, acknowledgment of sin, and acknowledgment of the character of God, but preoccupation with *relief* from the pain of the sin while continuing to practice the sin (Ex. 9:27-35).
E. Sorrow over sin yet seeking to handle the consequences of the sin according to our *will* instead of God's way (Matt. 27:3-5).

IV. There are certain indicators of godly sorrow (what we call contrite sorrow). As we see these things manifest, we are watching genuine repentance take place. Repentance is the act of changing one's mind, resulting in a change of action toward sin. It is seeing sin from God's perspective, resulting in a change of purpose and life away from the sin (v11).

A. *Earnestness*—It is a sense of urgency or a diligence to turn away from that which is sinful and walk in that which is right in the sight of God.
B. *Vindication of ourselves*—It is making sure that the record has been set straight in the matter, the clearing of self as a result of being forgiven.
C. *Indignation*—The person has a hatred or disgust with the sin that has been committed. It gives the indication that a person is bothered by the sin or hates the sin as God hates it.

D. *Fear*—The person is afraid of the wrath of God. It suggests that there is a fear of the discipline of the Lord and a healthy awareness that God deals with us in our sin.
E. *Longing*—There is a desire for reconciliation and connection with God and a right relationship with God.
F. *Zeal*—The person shows a passion for seeing things done right in accordance to God's will and for God's will to be done in a specific matter.
G. *Avenging of wrong*—The person makes sure justice is done. In the context of the passage, avenging wrong has to do with seeing justice done for the sin that was committed. A person who is truly repentant will seek to avenge the wrong.
H. *Innocent in the matter*—seeking to be clean of the sin which one has committed. One is pursuing holiness in the matter. Therefore to seek to be innocent in a matter is to seek to be pure or clean.

V. The Practice of Repentance (Eph. 4:22-24)

A. Identify where we may have been thinking, speaking, or acting in sin toward God in particular situations (Ezra 10:1-2).
B. Identify where we may have been thinking, speaking, or acting in sin toward others in particular situations (Gen. 50:15-21).
C. Identify where we may have been thinking, speaking, or acting in sin in response to unfavorable or difficult circumstances (Ps. 73:1-22).
D. Identify what we want or desire that we cannot control getting from God, others, or circumstances (Jas. 3:13-4:3).
E. Confess and repent of lusting after those wants or desires we cannot control getting from God, others, or circumstances (Prov. 28:13-14).
F. Confess and repent of ungodly thoughts, words, or actions toward God, others, and circumstances (Ps. 32:1-11, Jas. 5:16).
G. Identify the thoughts, words, actions, or desires God is seeking to develop through our circumstances (Jas. 1:1-8, 1 Peter 1:1-9).
H. Discipline ourselves to think, behave, and relate in ways that are pleasing to God (Phil. 3:7-21, Eph. 4:17-32).
I. Identify various ways we can show thanks to God for what He is allowing in our lives (1 Thess. 5:18, Prov. 17:22).
J. Lay out a daily schedule of tasks that we are responsible for doing and work on accomplishing them apart from our feelings (Prov. 16:1,3,9, 24:27).

K. Identify some key ways you can serve others and do it apart from your feelings (Rom. 12:3-21, 1 Peter 4:10-11).
L. Focus on speaking words that are edifying (Eph. 4:29).
M. Learn to receive and cultivate hope that comes from trusting God (Rom. 5:1-5, Heb. 6:9-20, 1 Peter 1:13-16, Heb. 12:1-3, 1 John 3:1-3).

SECTION 14

Forgiveness

Key Point: The more we count on the fact of how forgiven we are, the greater and deeper our forgiveness will be for others. Once we see how wretched we are and how much we are forgiven, the more we are inclined to forgive others. However, we must not confuse forgiving people with loving people (Eph. 4:32, Luke 17:3-4, Matt. 18:15-18,21-35, 1 John 1:9, Ps. 32:1-5, Gal. 6:1-2).

Definition of forgiveness: To disregard, to let go of, to release from, to pardon, and to cancel a debt owed

I. What we must consider about sin and forgiveness (Rom. 5:6-11):

A. Forgiveness of sin is possible because of the sacrifice of Jesus Christ; He paid the penalty for our sins. He made the sacrifice of His life for the saving of ours from the penalty of sin (Rom. 5:6-11, 6:23, 1 John 2:1-2).

B. Forgiveness of sin results in the judicial act of people being made legally right with God forever; their sins no longer count against them as it relates to damnation. God is no longer angry with them. They are reconciled to a right relationship with God—Judicial Forgiveness/Reconciliation (Rom. 5:1, 6-11).

C. Once people are judicially set free from the penalty of sin, they still have to deal with God in their daily actions of sin that hinder their fellowship with God. Until people confess and repent of this sin in their daily life, they are unable to walk in fellowship with God and walk in love toward others since they are in the flesh. When confession and repentance take place, forgiveness of sin takes place, resulting in restoration of proper fellowship with God—Parental Forgiveness (1 John 1:9, Matt. 18:21-35, Prov. 28:13, Ps. 32:3-5).

D. Since Jesus paid the penalty for all sins committed by humanity, the penalty for sin has been satisfied through Him. But if people refuse to accept Christ's payment for sin, they will not receive forgiveness of their sin and have to pay for their own sin (1 John 2:1-2, John 3:16-18, Rom. 6:23).

II. The implications of sin and forgiveness (Ephesians 4:32):

A. Forgiveness of sin is available to all but not granted until people deal with their sin accordingly (Ps. 32:1-5, 1 John 3:8-12, Matt. 6:14-15, Luke 15:11-32).
B. God loves unconditionally but He grants forgiveness of sin on the basis of confession and repentance (Rom. 5:8, Prov. 28:13, Ps. 32:1-5, James 5:16).
C. We can love others unconditionally but we cannot grant forgiveness of sin to others until the sin is confessed and repented of (Luke 6:27-36, Rom. 12:9-21, Matt. 18:15-17).
D. Sin must be confronted, confessed, and repented of before it is forgiven (Gal. 6:1-2, Matt. 18:15-17, 2 Sam. 12:1-15).
E. Based upon the insights above, we can clearly see the application of Luke 17:1-4.

III. Sin issues are inevitable; therefore we need to be on guard (Luke 17:1-3).

A. We cannot avoid people trying to lead us into sin or sinning against us.
B. It would be bad for us if we are the stumbling block to others in this way, since it will bring negative consequences to our lives.
C. We need to watch ourselves and help keep others from becoming a stumbling block.
D. We need to identify where we are stumbling blocks and help others identify where they are stumbling blocks.

IV. We need to deal with sin issues and forgiveness accordingly (Luke 17:3-4).

A. We must confront clear sin lovingly before it can be forgiven.
B. If clear sin is confessed and repented of, it can then be forgiven.
C. As long as the sin is confessed and repented of, it does not matter how often it happens. It must be forgiven and put up with patiently.
D. If there is no confession and repentance of the sin, there can be no forgiveness of the sin. The sin issue must then be taken before witnesses and ultimately before the church leadership if not confessed and repented of before witnesses.

Ten-Step Guide to Dealing with Sin and Forgiveness

I. Before someone confronts another about an issue, he/she must determine if it is a personal preference issue, expectation issue, or clear sin before approaching the person (Prov. 13:3).

II. If it is a personal preference issue or expectation issue, confrontation may not need to happen because no sin has occurred—only disappointment and denial of a particular desire. Dealing with preferences and expectations is the issue. This must be considered personally to determine if it even needs to be addressed since it is not a sin issue (Rom. 14:1-22).

III. A person must identify all unloving thoughts, words, and actions within self in response to the preference issue, expectation issue, or clear sin, and confess and repent of all unloving thoughts, words, and actions to God and to others when appropriate (Prov. 28:13).

IV. After dealing with self, a person must confront the other about clear sin with the intent to restore him or her, not with the intent to destroy (Luke 17:3-4, Gal. 6:1-2, Prov. 27:6a, 1 Thess. 5:15).

V. If the person confesses and repents of the sin, forgive her/him (Luke 17:3-4).

VI. If the person confesses and repents of the sin, dismiss it and never bring it up again (Luke 17:3, 1 Peter 4:8).

VII. If the person refuses to confess and repent of the sin, bring witnesses to address it (Matt. 18:15-17).

VIII. If the person refuses to confess and repent of the sin with witnesses, take it to the leadership of the church so that they can address it (Matt. 18:15-17).

IX. No matter what the reaction of the other person or the outcome of the situation, one should be an open channel of love to the person (Luke 6:27-36).

X. A person should pray and do well to the offender (Luke 6:27-36, Rom. 12:14, 20-21, 1 Peter 3:9).

SECTION 15

A Biblical Perspective on Emotions

This section prompted by ideas from Thomson, 2112

I. Definition of <u>emotion</u>

A. The word *emotion* originated from the Latin *emovere* (e-, out + *movere*, move).
B. It means to "stir up," and these stirrings move one to action or decision.

II. The world's view of emotions

A. The world sees emotions as a product of human evolutionary history.
B. Emotions are viewed as unwilled thoughts and reactions to circumstances that are predetermined by biological processes of the body (Berger, 2019, 77).
C. Emotions are seen as originating out of the physical body.

III. The biblical view of emotions

A. The Bible describes emotions as having their origin in a non-physical, immaterial aspect of human nature, demonstrating that humans are created in the image of God.
B. God is Spirit (John 4:24) and has no physical brain or body. In His very nature He possesses qualities which are consistently regarded by human wisdom as emotions. Examples: Love (1 John 4:8, 16), Jealousy (Nahum 1:2), Anger (Heb. 3:10), Hatred (Ps. 5:5), Joy (Zeph. 3:17, Sorrow (Eph. 4:30).
C. Not only does God possess emotions apart from a material existence, His Word also teaches that He has created humans in His own image (Gen. 1:26) with an immaterial aspect to their nature in which we also experience emotion. Examples: Godly/Sinful Hatred (Ps. 105:25, Lev. 19:17), Anger (Eccl. 7:9, 11:10), Envy (Prov. 23:17), Fear (John 14:27, Is. 35:4), Joy (Ps. 13:5, John 16:22), Sorrow (John 16:6, Rom. 9:2).
D. Emotions from a biblical perspective can be described as sensations of the soul that occur as a result of the thoughts and attitudes of the mind, thereby also exposing the values, desires, and motivations associated with those thoughts and attitudes of the mind.
E. "In a sense, emotions are the empirical evidence of the soul's existence and its executive control over the body" (Berger, 2019, 173).

IV. God's judgment of emotions

A. Emotions of animals originate in their brains and bodies; they have no immaterial nature in which they are responsible to God.

B. Humans, on the other hand, have an immaterial nature, and according to Scripture, most of human emotions originate in that nature.

C. God weighs as right or wrong those moral attitudes in a person's life which determine the emotions. God does not judge the experience of the emotions themselves as right or wrong, but He does weigh the heart attitudes that initiate them (1 Cor. 4:5, Jer. 17:10, Heb. 4:12).

D. Emotions prove or demonstrate that humans have a value/moral system within the fabric of human immaterial nature (Berger, 2019, 183).

V. The three areas where emotions originate

A. *Attitude*—Human emotions originate as a thought or a system of thoughts in a person's immaterial heart, which then are experienced as sensations in his/her immaterial heart, physical brain, and physical body. Examples: Grief (Matt. 26:36-38), Disappointment (Prov. 13:12), Agony (Luke 22:44).

B. *Conscience*—Human emotions originate as thoughts of warnings or affirmations of the conscience upon people's right or wrong attitudes, words, and actions. The conscience excuses or accuses them (Rom. 2:14-15), which in turn stimulates the sensations they experience in their immaterial heart, physical brain, and physical body from the excusing and accusing of the conscience. Examples: Bothered conscience (1 Sam. 24:5), Troubled conscience (2 Sam. 24:10), Confidence (1 John 3:21).

C. *Physiological*—Human emotions originate in a person's material brain as thoughts of warnings of possible physical danger, or thoughts of pain or pleasure being experienced as sensations in the body connected to the physical nerve endings. Examples: Startle or Fright (Ruth 3:8), Pleasure (Prov. 21:17), Affliction (2 Cor. 4:8).

Emotions

God is Spirit; He has emotions.
We are created in His image.

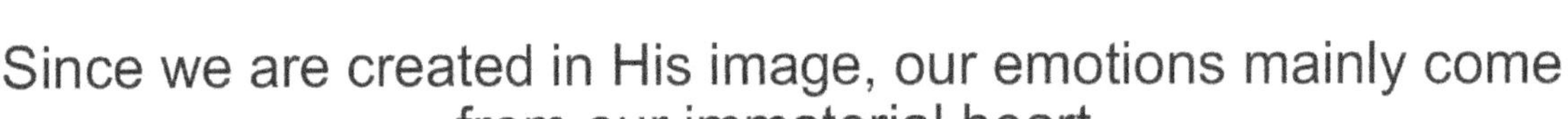

Since we are created in His image, our emotions mainly come from our immaterial heart.

Our thoughts/attitudes determine what we feel; they determine our emotions.

Therefore, our emotions are a by-product of our thoughts/attitudes.

These emotions derive from three areas:

a. A person's mind produces attitudes that produce emotions.

b. The conscience produces attitudes (right or wrong) that produce emotions.

c. The brain produces warnings, resulting in the emotions of startle or fright as well as pleasure or pain.

Since emotions come from our immaterial heart—

There is no such thing as damaged emotions, because emotions are the window to the thoughts and attitudes of our hearts.

We cannot be emotionally abused by others, because our emotions/feelings are a by-product of what we are thinking. We decide what we will think, which determines our emotions/feelings.

We control our emotions by controlling our thoughts/attitudes because emotions come from what we are thinking. If we control our thinking we control our emotions/feelings.

No one can determine what we feel because our feelings/emotions come from our thoughts/attitudes. Therefore, no one hurts our feelings. We have feelings/emotions of hurt because of what we are thinking about the person who disappointed us or sinned against us.

As a result, we cannot blame anyone for our feelings/emotions. The way we choose to think determines the way we feel or the emotions we have.

VI. Examples of each of these kinds of emotions

A. Attitude emotions

1. *Neutral attitude emotions*: common joy, common sorrow, amusement, delight, ecstasy, elation, enjoyment, euphoria, happiness, grief, anguish of heart, discomfort, displeasure, distress (when distress simply means troubled, not hopelessness), loneliness (when the reference is to one's relationship with other people), sadness, sorrow, uneasiness, unhappiness, embarrassment, regret
2. *Moral attitude emotions:* benevolence, contentment, empathy, gratitude, love, pity, sympathy, aggression, agitation (where it does not simply mean physical discomfort), anger, annoyance, fury, hate, hostility, irritation, rage, vexation, anxiety, apprehension, distress (when this means worry), dread, fear, terror, worry, dejection, depression, distress (not physically referenced), gloom, hopelessness (not only a Moral Attitude Emotion but, interestingly, also a Conscience-Stimulated Attitude Emotion to be discussed later), envy, jealousy, contempt, pride, self-pity, ingratitude, thanklessness, passivity, submission, confidence
3. *Situational moral attitude emotions:* (neutral attitude emotions that are used in a loving or unloving way): taking *pleasure* in wickedness, *rejoicing* in the suffering of the wicked, rejoicing in the repentance of sin, grief over not being able to sin as we want

B. **Conscience emotions**: sense of guilt, the sense of apparently uncaused fear (fear of judgment), the sense of peace, the sense of confidence before God, bothered conscience, troubled conscience

C. **Physiological emotions**: startled, frightened, bodily pain, bodily pleasure

VII. What role should a counselor allow a counselee's emotions to play in counseling?

A. Counseling should evaluate the emotions being presented by others as a means to determine the attitudes of a counselee's heart.

B. Since we know that emotions stem from attitudes, the key would be to learn the attitude to change through evaluating the emotions being presented.

VIII. How can we tell the difference between sinful emotions and righteous emotions?

A. Sinful emotions in essence are sinful attitudes being displayed through the emotion. Righteous emotions in essence are righteous attitudes being displayed through the emotion.
B. Therefore, we evaluate the emotion according to the character of it. (See VI above.)

IX. How would a counselor use Scripture to help a counselee change improper emotions?

A. Identify the attitude that is determining the emotion.
B. Then lead the person to realize, remorse, renounce, and repent of the sinful attitude behind the emotion.
C. Then lead the person to renew her/his mind in the right attitude and replace the sinful attitude with the right attitude, resulting in proper emotions.

SECTION 16

Distinguishing Between the Various Types of Fears Mentioned in the Bible

I. The Bible mentions a kind of fear that is not sinful; it is neutral. It is a fear that has a definite *external cause*. It can be traced to something specific externally. An example is startle or fright, an instantaneous and instinctual response to possible bodily danger (Ruth 3:8, Luke 24:37).

II. The Bible mentions another set of fears that are good and right. These kinds of fears also have a definite *external cause*. They can be traced to something specific externally. These kinds of fears are consistent with loving and trusting God.

A. Fear that is described as *reverence* for the Lord is consistent with loving and trusting God (Prov. 1:7).
B. Fear that is described as *concern* is consistent with loving and trusting God (Gal. 4:11).
C. Fear that is described as *respect* is consistent with loving and trusting God (Rom. 13:7, 1 Peter 3:2).

III. The Bible mentions another set of fears that are wrong and sinful. These kinds of fears have a definite *external cause*, which can be traced to something specific externally. These fears are inconsistent with loving and trusting God.

A. Having a fear of *false gods* is inconsistent with loving and trusting God (Jer. 10:2-5).
B. Being *worried* is a fear that is inconsistent with loving and trusting God (Luke 12:4-7, 32).
C. Being timid, cowardly, or *intimidated* is a fear that is inconsistent with loving and trusting God (2 Tim. 1:7, Joshua 1:9, Prov. 29:25).

IV. The Bible mentions another kind of fear that is the by-product of internal guilt. It does not have a discernable *external cause* but is traced solely to *internal guilt.* It is called the fear of God's *judgment*. This is commonly known and called anxiety. Psychologists define anxiety as a fear with no discernable external cause. They observe that it comes and goes for no external reason. There is no external apparent cause because it is a by-product of a guilty conscience, yet they would deny this reality.

A. The fear of God's *judgment* is seen in Adam when he sinned; it was not caused by anything external but was a by-product of his guilty conscience as the result of his sin choice (Gen. 3:1-10).
B. The fear of God's *judgment* is seen when people are running and no one is chasing them. The fear is not caused by anything external but is a by-product of a guilty conscience as the result of making a sin choice (Prov. 28:1, Lev. 26:17, 36-37).
C. The fear of God's *judgment* is not like any of the other fears, because it is not something we control by choice but is the by-product of a choice. We don't deal with the fear of God's judgment through actually dealing with the fear (or what psychologists call anxiety). We deal with it through confessing our sins (Ps. 32:1-5, Prov. 28:13).

The Fear of Worry vs. the Fear of God's Judgment (Anxiety)

Built on concepts from Rich Thomson

The Fear of Worry	The Fear of God's Judgment (Anxiety)
The fear is attached to a visible issue.	The fear is not attached to a visible issue.
The fear is in proportion to the threat.	The fear is out of proportion to the threat.
The root of the problem is not trusting God with the issues.	The root of the problem involves an unloving attitude, words, or actions, and the person is unable to see that it is producing the fear that seems to come out of nowhere.
Counseling focuses on trusting God with the thing the person is fearful about.	Counseling focuses on finding the root unloving attitude, word, or action that is producing the fear that seems to come out of nowhere, so that the person may confess, count on forgiveness, be controlled by the Holy Spirit, and count on the control of the Holy Spirit as he/she walks in love in that area. This helps her/him overcome the fear that seems to come out of nowhere.
The fear comes and goes as troubles come and go.	The fear hangs on whether troubles are present or not; it's difficult to understand why it disappears when it does.
A person should confess this fear as sin.	A person should identify the sin that is producing the fear that seems to come out nowhere, because the fear is the result of that sin, not sin itself.

SECTION 17

Understanding Anger

I. The <u>definition</u> of *anger* (Eph. 4:26-32)

A. Disposition of the mind that entertains antagonism toward another individual, manifesting itself in various emotions and actions (Gen. 4:1-8, Mark 3:1-6).

B. Anger is an attitude that results in emotions that move into action (Prov. 14:17,29, 15:18, 16:32, 19:19, 22:24-25).

C. Anger can be godly/righteous indignation—to be troubled or disgusted in attitude or action as a result of someone disgracing God or disregarding His holy laws (Ex. 32:1-30, Eph. 4: 26-27, John 2:12-17, Neh. 5:1-13).

D. Anger can be worldly/sinful—to have ungodly attitudes and actions as a result of some perceived need, desire, personal preference/standard not being met by someone or being offended by someone (Num. 20:1-13, Eph. 4:31-32, 1 Sam. 18:6-8, 20:24-34; Jas. 1:19-20, Matt. 5:21-22).

II. The <u>deliberation</u> on righteous indignation vs. worldly/sinful anger (Eph. 4:26-32)

A. Godly anger or righteous indignation is the exception to the rule. Very seldom when people are angry is it about the things that disgrace God or disregard His holy laws. When they walk in righteous indignation, they are filled with a desire to see justice done for the glory of God (not self) as they are walking by the Spirit of God in this kind of anger. When people do act in godly anger or righteous indignation, they are commanded to deal with it before the day is over so that the devil does not use it against them to lead them into sin.

B. Generally, when people are angry it has nothing to do with someone disgracing God or disregarding His holy laws. They are not thinking about God, His holy laws, His righteousness, His will, or His ways. They are thinking about themselves, their feelings, their wants, or their needs. They are self-centered, not God-centered. They are preoccupied with what they crave, the means to the end that is not providing that craving, or something that is hindering that craving from being realized.

C. Therefore, most of the time when people are angry, it is generally human, worldly/sinful anger. What they want within the situation is not granted, or they are receiving something they do not want or they are not receiving what they want.
D. As a result of not receiving what they want or getting what they don't want, ungodly attitudes and actions begin to manifest. Instead of being thankful to God for how He will use the situation or accepting what God has allowed in the situation, they become negative and ungodly in thoughts, words, actions, and relational patterns.

III. The <u>details</u> of life that can lead to worldly/sinful anger

A. Worldly/sinful anger may occur as a result of misplaced dependence: depending on people, places, things, or events to provide what only God provides.
B. Worldly/sinful anger may occur as a result of unrealistic expectations: expecting things that are beyond the scope of possibility.
C. Worldly/sinful anger may occur as a result of being untrained in handling disappointments: not accepting the fallibility of people, places, things, and events.
D. Worldly/sinful anger may occur as a result of not accepting powerlessness over people, places, outcomes of events: resisting the fact that we were not designed to control people and the outcome of events.

IV. The <u>desires</u> that become <u>demands</u> of the heart and the source of worldly/sinful anger (Jas. 4:1-2)

A. When the desire to be affirmed becomes a demand to be affirmed, worldly/sinful anger results when our demands are not met.
B. When the desire not to be put down by others becomes a demand not to be put down by others, worldly/sinful anger results when our demands are not met.
C. When the desires that are centered on things of this life become a demand for things of this life, worldly/sinful anger results when our demands are not met:
D. We walk in worldly/sinful anger of man when we demand__________ and do not get it:

1. To have control, To be loved, To be accepted, To be understood
2. To never hurt again, To be respected, To be served, To have our way
3. To be viewed as competent, To be approved of, To belong to someone
4. To be held in high regard, To maintain a favorable position with people

E. When the desire for people to do or handle things our way or for life to go our way becomes a demand, worldly/sinful anger of man results when our demands are not met.

V. The <u>different</u> expressions of worldly/sinful anger (Eph. 4:31)

A. Bitterness—resentment
B. Wrath—intense fury or rage
C. Anger—deep-seated hostility within the heart toward another
D. Clamor—verbal fighting with people / Slander—ugly words, mean words or verbal abuse in reference to someone's reputation

VI. The <u>dangerous</u> ways people deal with anger (Jas. 1:19-20, Eph. 4:26-27)

A. Suppression—acting like it does not exist
B. Aggression—openly expressed anger at someone else's expense
C. Passive Aggressive—indirectly expressed anger at someone else's expense
D. Not dealing with it before the day is done

VII. The <u>direction</u> to deal with anger (Jas. 1:19, Eph. 4:31, Col. 3:1-8)

A. Acknowledge our anger
B. Confess the sin of our anger
C. Identify the details of life whereby we have chosen to be angry
D. Identify the specific desires we have been demanding to be fulfilled by God, people, places, and events—resulting in responding in anger as a result of not getting our way
E. Accept our inability to control God, people, and the outcome of circumstances
F. Accept these conditions:

1. The person may be willing and able
2. The person may be willing and unable
3. The person may be unwilling and able
4. The person may be unwilling and unable
5. It may be a desire that was not meant to be satisfied

G. Accept responsibility for our unloving thoughts, words, deeds in the situation
H. Repent of unloving thoughts, words, deeds in the situation
I. Choose to serve and love others unconditionally

J. Follow the biblical mandate according to the relationship (1 Cor. 13:4-7)

1. Husband/Wife (Eph. 5:18-33, Col. 3:18-19, 1 Peter 3:1-12)
2. Children (Eph. 6:1-2, Col. 3:20)
3. Parent (Eph. 6:4, Col. 3:21, Deut. 6:6-9, Prov. 22:6)
4. Friends (Prov. 27:5-6, 9; 17:17; 18:24)
5. Others (1 Peter 3:8-12, Rom. 12:9-21, Gal. 6:1-10)
6. Leaders (1 Tim. 4:16, Heb. 13:7, 17; 1 Peter 5:5, 1 Tim. 5:17-22, Luke 6:40)
7. Employer/Employee (Eph. 6:5-9, 1 Peter 2:18-29)
8. Government (Rom.13:1-2, 1 Peter 2:13-17)
9. Enemies (Luke 6:27-36)

K. Don't allow anger to go beyond that day (Eph. 4:26-27)

SECTION 18

Understanding and Dealing with Depression

I. The <u>characterization</u> of depression: The experience of deep sorrow, hopelessness, and a sense of guilt connected to one's beliefs, way of life, expectations, and reactions toward God, self, people, life in general, and circumstances in specific.

II. The <u>cause</u> of depression

A. Depression can result from unbiblical thinking, unbiblical living, and unbiblical responses (Ps. 73:1-22, 38:1-18; Gen. 4:1-14, Lam. 1:20).

B. Depression can arise from wrong views: of God, of self, of people, of life in general, and of circumstances in specific.

C. Depression can also arise from dealing with God, self, people, life in general, and circumstances in specific in ways that the Bible defines as sin.

III. The <u>confusion</u> about depression

A. Depression should not be confused with deep sorrow. Deep sorrow is the normal response to disappointment, difficulty, or even devastating life issues that are not accompanied with corresponding sin in thoughts and actions, while experiencing a sense of peace (Ps. 34:8, Prov. 13:12, 2 Kings 4:8-37).

B. However, depression is a combination of deep sorrow, hopelessness, and a sense of guilt that is the result of sin in thoughts and actions (Ps. 38:1-18, 73:1-22; Gen. 4:1-14).

C. We can have deep sorrow without hopelessness and a sense of guilt while experiencing a sense of peace. However, we will not have depression without hopelessness and a sense of guilt. The experience of depression is not sin itself but the result thereof (Prov. 13:12, Ps. 73:1-22).

IV. The cure for depression

A. Identify where we may have been thinking, speaking, or acting in sin toward God in particular situations (Ezra 10:1-2).
B. Identify where we may have been thinking, speaking, or acting in sin toward others in particular situations (Gen. 50:15-21).
C. Identify where we may have been thinking, speaking, or acting in sin in response to unfavorable or difficult circumstances (Ps. 73:1-22).
D. Identify what we want or desire that we cannot control getting from God, others, or circumstances (Jas. 3:13-4:3).
E. Confess and repent of lusting after those wants or desires we cannot control getting from God, others, or circumstances (Prov. 28:13-14).
F. Confess and repent of ungodly thoughts, words, or actions towards God, others, and circumstances (Ps. 32:1-11, Jas. 5:16).
G. Identify the thoughts, words, actions, or desires God is seeking to develop through our circumstances (Jas. 1:1-8, 1 Peter 1:1-9).
H. Discipline ourselves to think, behave, and relate in ways that are pleasing to God (Phil. 3:7-21, Eph. 4:17-32).
I. Identify various ways we can show thanks to God for what He is allowing in our lives (1Thess. 5:18, Prov. 17:22).
J. Lay out a daily schedule of tasks that we are responsible for doing and work on accomplishing them apart from our feelings (Prov. 16:1,3,9; 24:27).
K. Identify some key ways we can serve others and do it apart from our feelings (Rom. 12:3-21, 1 Peter 4:10-11).
L. Focus on speaking words that are edifying (Eph. 4:29).
M. Learn to receive and cultivate hope that comes from trusting God (Rom. 5:1-5, Heb. 6:9-20, 12:1-3; 1 Peter 1:13-16, 1 John 3:1-3).

V. Six Questions to Consider in Evaluating Our Situation

A. What is it that God wants me to come to embrace about Him in this situation?
B. What is the biblical view of this situation?
C. What does God want me to see about myself in this situation?
D. What does God want me to learn about others in this situation?
E. What does God want me to do in this situation?
F. What will be my future service to others as a result of doing what God wants me to do in this situation?

SECTION 19

A Biblical View and Response to Physical Illness and Christians on Psychotropic Drugs

Key Point: Illness is a by-product of the curse of sin from the Fall of Adam and the result of sin in our life, yet God can use it for His glory and our good. When we have an illness, there is something wrong in the tissues of our body that can be proven by objective tests. Mental illness is really not an illness but truly an issue of the immaterial heart that needs to be addressed through the Person of Jesus Christ, the power of Jesus Christ, and the principles of His Word. There may be physical issues that result from the spiritual problem that may require medication, but the root issue cannot be cured through medication but only through submission to the Person and power of Jesus Christ. Genuine biblical counseling operates by this premise. It does not promote medication where the Messiah is needed. Genuine biblical counseling discerns between pain that comes from the immaterial nature and pain that comes from the material nature.

I. The biblical view of physical illness

A. Illness exists because of the Fall of Adam, which resulted in the curse of sin on our lives, leading to weak and frail bodies (Rom. 5:12, 1 Peter 1:24).
B. Illness may occur due to unconfessed sin in our lives (Ps. 32:1-4).
C. Illness may occur because God is punishing an unbeliever (Ex. 15:26).
D. Illness may occur because God is disciplining a believer (2 Sam. 12:14-15).
E. Illness may occur because God is seeking to bring about repentance (1 Cor. 5:5).
F. Illness may occur because God is using it to prevent a person from sinning (2 Cor. 12:7).
G. Illness may occur as a natural consequence of not taking care of our bodies as designed (Prov. 19:16).
H. Illness may occur as a result of unbiblical thinking and actions (2 Chron. 26:19).
I. Illness can be used by God to bring glory to Himself (John 11:1-4).
J. Illness can be used by God to expose the character of a person (Job 2:1-6).

II. Key perspectives to consider for the person struggling with a physical illness

A. There must be biblical understanding of physical illness (Rom. 12:2).
B. God has the physical illness under His sovereign control (Eccl. 7:13-14).
C. God will not allow physical illness to rise above what we can handle (1 Cor. 10:13).
D. God will give what is needed so we can function as God commanded in spite of the physical sickness (2 Cor. 9:8).
E. God wants us to be victorious, not victims in our responses to physical sickness (1 Cor. 15:57, Job 1:1-2:10).

III. An approach to help people with physical illness

A. Help the counselees to see God's perspective on illness.
B. Help the counselees to focus more on becoming like Christ as the primary goal and getting over the illness as the secondary goal.
C. Teach the counselees how to use God's grace to function responsibly even when they feel horrible.
D. Teach the counselees how to be thankful even when they feel terrible.
E. Teach the counselees to focus on victory above relief.

IV. Key points to consider about Christians on psychotropic drugs: *psycho* (mind)+-*tropic* (affecting) = mind altering/affecting drugs

A. Christians who are on psychotropic drugs may be focused more on feeling better through the medication than becoming better through the biblical process of change.
B. Christians who use psychotropic drugs may not understand how to use the Bible to find God's solution to life's problems; therefore they are left to secular understanding about their problems, resulting in using psychotropic drugs as the solution.
C. Christians who use psychotropic drugs may be treated by professionals who deal only in psychotropic drugs to address the particular issues at hand.
D. Christians who use psychotropic drugs may believe that they cannot obey God when they feel bad; therefore they may believe that the only time they can be responsible is when they feel good by the use of medication.
E. Christians who use psychotropic drugs may have been told that their problems are based on physical conditions of the body that require medication.

F. Christians who use psychotropic drugs may not trust in the sufficiency of Scripture to handle their problems.
G. Christians who use psychotropic drugs may not understand or accept why and how God uses pain and trials to build character.

V. Biblical perspectives to consider about Christians and psychotropic drugs

A. The Bible is sufficient to provide everything we need for life and godliness, which includes bad feelings that people try to address through psychotropic drugs instead of the Messiah and His Word (2 Peter 1:1-11, 2 Tim. 3:16-17).
B. God's goal for our lives is not that we live to feel better but that we live to become better through the biblical process of change (Eph. 4:17-32, Col. 3:1-17).
C. When there is no organic basis found for discomfort or pain, we will find that unbiblical responses to life's situations are the core reasons for the discomfort/pain; therefore psychotropic drugs may deal with the pain of discomfort but not with the source of the discomfort (unbiblical responses) (Gen. 4:1-7, Rom. 2:14-15).
D. Sinful behavior and the bad feelings that follow do not come from organic problems of the body; sinful behavior comes from the wickedness of the heart. The bad feelings that follow come from the conscience that stimulates the sense of guilt, apparently uncaused fear, and the desire to flee when no one is chasing. Therefore psychotropic drugs are not the cure; the Messiah and His Word are the cure (Matt. 15:11-20, Mark 7:20-23, 2 Cor. 5:11-17).
E. Psychotropic drugs will make us *feel* better but they will not help us to *become* better (Gal. 5:16,19-26, Gen. 4:1-7, Rom. 7:4-8:15).
F. Medication is a great support but a terrible solution to nonorganic problems (Prov. 31:4-7).

Distinguishing Physical and Spiritual Pain

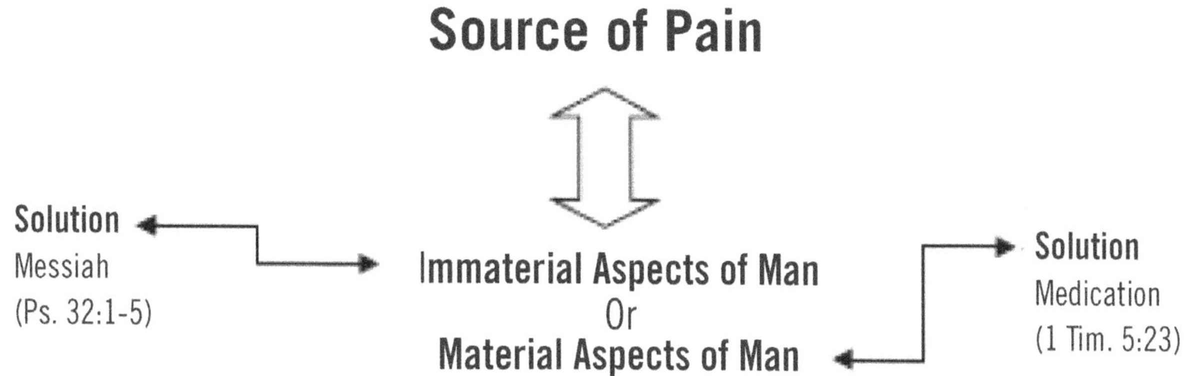

False Belief about Medication and Obedience

Pain < Obedience (Lesser the pain / greater my obedience)

Pain > Obedience (Greater the pain / lesser my obedience)

Therefore, medication is necessary for me to obey God.

False Conclusion: Medication brings relief of pain, resulting in a person's feeling better and being able to obey because of feeling better due to the medication.

Fallacy: A person believes that the power to obey is caused by feeling better as the result of taking the medication.

Truth: The power to obey is determined by the Holy Spirit, not by feeling better as a result of taking medication. Pain or lack of pain does not determine obedience (Rom. 8:1-15, Gal. 5:16-25).

VI. An approach to help Christians on psychotropic drugs

A. Help the counselees identify the specific situations and problems that were happening to them, around them, or through them that led to the taking of psychotropic drugs.

B. Help the counselees identify the responses and reactions that took place from them in correlation to the specific situations and problems that led to the taking of psychotropic drugs.

C. Help the counselees to identify the negative feelings that arose and how they chose to handle those negative feelings in correlation to the specific situations and problems.

D. Help the counselees to identify their goals, whether biblical or self-serving, in the specific situations and problems.
E. Help the counselees identify their goals for taking the psychotropic drugs in the specific situations and problems.
F. Help the counselees to interpret life through biblical categories in correlation to their specific situations and problems.
G. Help the counselees to apply biblical principles to the specific situations and problems so that they will focus more on being like Christ instead of feeling better in the crisis.
H. Help the counselee to focus on becoming a better person through application of biblical principles to the specific situations and problems instead of feeling better in the specific situations and problems.
I. Coming off the medication is not the goal, but helping the person to handle the specific situations and problems biblically is the goal.
J. As the counselees come to see that they can handle the specific situations and problems through the power of God and the principles of His Word, whether they feel bad or not, they will begin to work on coming off the medication as a secondary goal—as the counselor has helped them to develop in the primary goal of becoming like Christ and handling situations biblically as they walk for God and others.

Above information developed from concepts in The Christian Counselor's Medical Desk Reference *by Robert D. Smith, MD.*

SECTION 20

Addressing the Concept of Chemical Imbalance Biblically

I. The Bible teaches that humans are a unity of body and soul.

A. Mental health cannot be reduced to chemical processes in the brain; it has spiritual, emotional, and moral dimensions. Focusing on causes neglects the soul's role in human experience (Gen. 2:7).

B. Scripture emphasizes the heart as the center of human thinking, emotions, desires, and actions. Issues such as anxiety, depression, or anger are connected to the heart's response to life's challenges rather than merely brain chemistry (Prov. 4:23).

C. The fallen nature of humanity affects every part of human existence. Spiritual problems, including guilt, bitterness, or fear, stem from sin and are not biological issues that can be fixed with medicine (Rom. 3:23).

D. The Bible emphasizes renewing the mind through truth and transformation in Christ, demonstrating that mental struggles involve thought patterns that can be transformed by spiritual growth rather than chemical alteration (Rom. 12:2).

II. Scripture acknowledges that suffering, including emotional and mental distress, is part of life in a fallen world.

A. This suffering is not a matter of physical imbalance but can be used by God for spiritual growth and sanctification (Rom. 8:20-22).

B. The Bible teaches that worry can be alleviated by trusting in God, praying, and experiencing the peace that surpasses understanding. These are spiritual remedies for emotional distress that go beyond medical explanations (Phil. 4:6-7).

C. Scripture presents God as the ultimate healer of emotional and spiritual wounds, emphasizing that healing involves more than managing chemical levels but requires God's intervention in the heart and soul (Ps. 34:18).

D. The Bible holds individuals accountable for their words and actions, even in emotional or mental struggles, demonstrating that our emotional responses are not caused by brain chemistry but involve moral and spiritual accountability (Matt. 12:36-37).

E. Scripture cautions against relying on human wisdom, urging believers to seek God's wisdom, which often includes addressing heart issues, repentance, and spiritual growth rather than turning to physical solutions (1 Cor. 1:20).
F. Jesus invites those who are weary and burdened to find rest in Him. This rest is not found in medication or worldly solutions, but in the spiritual healing, transformation, and peace that Christ offers (Matt. 11:28-30).

III. The idea of a chemical imbalance has been heavily promoted by pharmaceutical companies.

A. This is a marketing strategy to sell psychotropic medications, rather than being based on strong scientific evidence.
B. No conclusive scientific evidence exists to prove that mental disorders are caused by specific chemical imbalances, such as deficiencies in serotonin.
C. Research shows that the effectiveness of antidepressants is largely attributed to the placebo effect rather than their ability to correct a chemical imbalance.

IV. Biblical counseling acknowledges the role of medical science in treating physical illnesses.

A. Medications can sometimes help alleviate physical symptoms (1 Tim. 5:23).
B. Instead of focusing on altering brain chemistry, biblical counseling emphasizes the need for addressing heart issues and finding renewal through Christ (Rom. 12:2).
C. When structural abnormalities in the brain are identified, they are typically classified as neurological disorders rather than psychiatric conditions, highlighting psychiatry's lack of biological foundation.
D. Brain chemicals are constantly fluctuating, and no "normal" balance has been established. Claims of chemical imbalances are speculative and lack measurable evidence.
E. Psychotropic medications, intended to correct imbalances, often create artificial disturbances in brain chemistry, potentially causing harm.
F. Research supporting the chemical imbalance theory is often influenced by pharmaceutical companies, raising concerns about conflicts of interest and biased study results.
G. Studies that manipulate serotonin levels have failed to confirm the chemical imbalance theory, showing no consistent connection between serotonin and depression.
H. Psychotropic drugs disrupt normal nervous system function instead of fostering healing, leading to various mental and physical side effects.

I. The biblical view prioritizes addressing the soul and heart issues at the core of human struggles.

V. Soul and heart issues are areas that medication cannot resolve.

A. Psychiatry's dependence on the chemical imbalance theory has been criticized as speculative and lacking credible evidence.
B. By focusing solely on biochemical causes, psychiatry often disregards the spiritual and relational components of human suffering, which are central to biblical counseling.
C. Scripture provides sufficient guidance for addressing emotional and spiritual challenges, emphasizing repentance, faith, and renewal rather than medicalization.
D. Lasting healing comes from Christ, who addresses the root issues of human struggles, such as sin and the need for reconciliation with God.

Summary: Biblical counseling takes physical health into account while prioritizing spiritual and emotional growth based on biblical principles. Both scientific and biblical perspectives call for transparency about the limitations of psychotropic medications and the speculative claims of the chemical imbalance theory. True peace, healing, and rest for the soul are found in Jesus Christ, not in medications or human theories (Matt. 11:28-30, John 14:27). While medication can sometimes assist in managing physical symptoms, genuine transformation comes through repentance, spiritual renewal, and the renewing of the mind.

For further understanding, read The Chemical Imbalance Delusion *by Dr. Daniel Berger II. Much of the research referenced here is based on his work.*

SECTION 21

Have You Considered the Purpose of Our Trials?

JAMES 1:1-8

I. Trials expose and develop our faith (v1-v3).

A. Expose *what* we depend on apart from God, so that we may turn from it and turn to God to build true hope in Him alone
B. Expose *who* we depend on apart from God, so that we may turn from them and turn to God to build true hope in Him alone
C. Expose *what* we truly believe about God in real time, so that we may make the necessary adjustments to build true hope in Him alone

II. Trials expose and develop our endurance (v3).

A. Expose how we handle *delays* and teach us how to persevere and stay godly as we work through them
B. Expose how we handle *denial* and teach us how to persevere and stay godly as we work through it
C. Expose how we handle *disruptions* and teach us how to persevere and stay godly as we work through them
D. Expose how we handle *devastations* and teach us how to persevere and stay godly as we work through them

III. Trials that are endured expose and develop our character (v4).

A. Expose our immature and *sinful* thoughts, words, actions, and expectations toward God and lead us to replace them by developing godly thoughts, words, actions, and expectations toward God
B. Expose our immature and *sinful* thoughts, words, actions, and expectations toward others and lead us to replace them by developing godly thoughts, words, actions, and expectations toward others

C. Expose our immature and *sinful* thoughts, words, actions, and expectations toward life and lead us to replace them by developing godly thoughts, words, actions, and expectations toward life

IV. Consider this about your trials (v5-v8).

A. If we humble ourselves before God, acknowledge that we need Him, and do not stubbornly insist on our own way, God will respond by giving us *divine* help to walk in His will through the trial (Berg, 2002).
B. If we don't believe that God will help us, we can't *expect* Him to.
C. If we don't believe that God will help us, we will be *indecisive* about our choices, *hesitant* in our choices, and *divided* in our choices as we go back and forth between trusting God and trusting ourselves.
D. If we don't believe that God will help us, we will live a life that is *unstable*, *complicated*, and *destructive*, because we know the truth of God's Word but live by the lies of Satan's world.

Key Points to Consider

I. Expectations not being realized can lead us to the end of ourselves and into building genuine *faith* in our Lord Jesus Christ, resulting in living a life prepared and prescribed by God with people and circumstances.

II. When we stop trying to fulfill our expectations through people and circumstances, we can begin to live for our *Savior* while living with others (2 Cor. 5:14-15).

III. When we stop trying to fulfill our expectations through people and circumstance, we can:

A. Learn how to enjoy the *pleasures* God provides through people and circumstances.
B. Learn how to endure the *pain* God allows through people and circumstances.
C. Submit to the *precepts* of God in His Word according to our roles and responsibilities with people and in circumstances.
D. Focus on and hold tightly to what God has *promised* within this life and the life to come.

E. Hold loosely in our hearts and hands what we would like to see, what we want, and what we would like to have happen that is not promised by God from *people and circumstances*, so that we can live a life of faith as prescribed and provided by God.

IV. Faith should be in

A. The *reality* of God.
B. The *reformation* of our existence in totality to reflect the character of Jesus Christ.
C. The *responsibility* of God to provide, protect, and prepare us for the next life.
D. The *rewards* of God in this life and the life to come.
E. The *return* of Christ and His glory along with the *residence* created by our Lord and Savior Jesus Christ when He returns for us.

V. Faith should not be in the realization of all of what we want through people and circumstances.

SECTION 22

God's Purpose for Marriage

The Purpose of Life

I. The <u>purpose</u> of life (Why do I exist?): We were created to bring *<u>glory</u>* to God in all aspects of life (Is. 43:7, Rom. 11:36, Col. 1:15-17, 1 Cor. 10:31, 2 Cor. 5:9,15, Matt. 5:14-16).

A. To glorify God and to demonstrate the greatness of His character
B. To demonstrate the greatness of His character by functioning according to His design in all aspects of life.
C. To demonstrate the greatness of His character by functioning according to His commands in all aspects of life.

II. The <u>objective</u> of life (What are the overarching goals I need to accomplish to fulfill my purpose?): We are to focus on <u>pleasing</u> God through seeking (2 Cor. 5:9,15):

A. To know God *<u>intimately</u>* (*Socialization with God*) (John 17:3).
B. To become like Jesus Christ to *<u>maturity</u>* in all aspects of life (*Sanctification in Jesus Christ)* (2 Cor. 3:18, Eph. 4:11-16).
C. To be *<u>useful</u>* to God (*Service for God*) (Eph. 2:10, Rom. 7:4, 1 Peter 4:10-11).

III. The <u>process</u> of life (What steps do we need to take to accomplish my goals to fulfill my purpose?): We must hear what to <u>obey</u> *and* then <u>obey</u> what we hear from God's Word in all aspects of life (Jas. 1:22-25, Prov. 3:5-7).

A. Learn the truth of God (2 Tim. 3:16, 2:15, Ps. 1:1-3, 119:104-105).
B. Live the truth of God we have learned (Jas. 1:19-22, Ps. 119:101-102).
C. Love others through the truth of God we have learned and are living (John 13:34-35, 1 Cor. 13:4-8, Eph. 4:16-17).

IV. The structure of life (How do we work this out in the context of life?) We must organize our lives around these particular roles and responsibilities:

A. We work this out in our role of *disciple*—We are to be followers of Christ and follow God's commands in all aspects of our lives (Matt. 28:18-20, John 8:31-36).

B. We work this out in our role of *ambassador*—As those who no longer belong to this world but to the Kingdom of God, we are to be an instrument in the hand of God whereby through our presenting the gospel of Jesus Christ, God may perhaps deliver sinners from their sin into a new and right relationship with God that will last for eternity (2 Cor. 5:11-21, 1 Cor. 3:5-9).

C. We work this out in our role of *builder*—As those who now are citizens of God's Kingdom and a part of His Church, we are to spend our lives helping other Christians grow to maturity in their character and faith in Jesus Christ (Eph. 4:11-16, Col. 1:28-29).

V. The way we should view ourselves

A. We have been created for the purpose of knowing God, reflecting the character of God, and being useful to God. Each person has been designed with material and nonphysical aspects so that he/she may function on earth as ordained and commanded by God.

B. God has control over humans and the entire universe. People were never designed to function outside of the moral commands of God.

C. The idea that people are at the center of our own existence, inherently good and able to determine our destiny apart from any need of God, directly contradicts the reality that all people are sinners in need of a Savior and cannot determine our destiny apart from the Creator who has set an agenda for each of us.

D. Ecclesiastes 9:1, Jeremiah 10:23, and Matthew 4:4 give us views of God as Sovereign Ruler, Sustainer, and Director of humanity in all aspects of existence. Therefore, we do not have the ability to know ourselves accurately, guide ourselves properly, grow ourselves, or sustain ourselves apart from God.

E. Any teaching that promotes self-dependency or even self-actualization is in contradiction to a biblical view of self-existence.

F. We must increasingly integrate into the Kingdom agenda of God at every point of our lives (Willard, 2009, 103-104). We must live our lives in interactive dependence upon God and interactive submission to His Kingdom rule (Titus 2:11-15) (Willard, 2009, 94).

Key Point: "We were never made or remade to live for ourselves. We were created for transcendence. The borders of our lives were always meant to be way bigger than the borders of our lives. When we live this way, by his grace, we not only become part of the most important work in the universe, but we are given back our humanity" (Tripp, 2007, 209-210).

God's Purpose for Marriage

I. God designed marriage for <u>companionship</u> (Gen. 2:18)

A. Marriage was designed so that man would not be alone.
B. Marriage was designed so that man would not be alone in fulfilling God's plan.
C. Marriage was designed for man and woman to be lifelong partners who would meet genuine needs of one another and satisfy legitimate desires of one another for life as priority above everyone else and everything else except God Himself (1 Cor. 7:33-34).

II. God designed marriage for <u>co-laboring</u> (Gen. 2:15-18)

A. Marriage was designed to provide man with a woman to assist him in his God-given responsibilities (Gen. 2:15-23).
B. Marriage was designed so that man and woman could work together as a team in fulfilling God's commandments accordingly (Gen. 1:26-28).
C. Marriage was designed to show how men and women can work together in a union to advance the Kingdom agenda of God (Gen. 1:27-28, 2:15-23).

III. God designed marriage for <u>cleaving</u> (Gen. 2:24)

A. Man and woman are called to come together as a family unit separate from their mothers and fathers.
B. Man and woman are called to come together and build a foundation based on their new family, not their original family.
C. Man and woman are called to come together to work on oneness in marriage.

IV. God designed marriage for completion (Gen. 2:24)

A. Marriage was designed so that man and woman can help each other come to know Jesus Christ intimately.
B. Marriage was designed so that man and woman can help each other become like Jesus Christ ultimately.
C. Marriage was designed so that man and woman can help each other become useful to Jesus Christ in practical ways, resulting in fulfilling their God-given purposes for existence.

V. God designed marriage to complement Christ and the Church (Eph 5:22-33)

A. Marriage is to reveal how Christ relates to the Church.
B. People are to see how Christ loves the Church as they see how a man loves his wife.
C. People are to see how the Church submits to Christ as they see how a woman submits to her husband.

SECTION 23

Understanding Manhood and the Role of the Husband

I. **The <u>definition</u> of a *<u>male</u>* (Hebrew: *zakar* /zaw·kawr): a human created by God as a spiritual and physical being—with a unique DNA and one X chromosome—for a particular function and purpose in the culture alongside and distinct from a female (woman) and all other creations of God (Gen. 1:27). In most cases men are born with a penis and testicles. In the event of either a lack of or an addition to his normal organs, a chromosome test should verify his gender.**

II. **The <u>definition</u> of *<u>manhood</u>* (Greek: *andrízomai* [to act manly]) (Kittel, 1985, 59): the mindset, manner, and movement that correspond distinctly to a male in form and function (1 Cor. 16:13). Manhood also refers to men who develop to the fullness of their being in courage: the mental and moral strength to resist opposition, handle danger, endure hardship, and to have firmness of mind and will in the face of danger or extreme difficulty while operating in a mindset, manner, and movement that is distinctly male, glorifying to God, and beneficial to others.**

III. **The <u>duties</u> of a male: These correspond with how he was created by God from the beginning to function (1 Cor. 11: 1-3):**

A. Men are responsible for taking the lead in *procreation* on earth by giving life through his seed to his wife only, to nurture that life to birth and beyond, so that humans would reflect the character of God throughout the earth (Gen. 1:26-30).

B. Men are responsible for taking the lead in *subduing the earth* by governing the earth with good stewardship, management, control, and order according to the will of God (Gen. 2:15, 19-20; 1:26-30).

C. Men are responsible for taking the lead in *dominion of the earth* by being a servant leader over creation and exercising authority, influence, and strength over creation and all who fall under their leadership for the glory of God and the good of creation (Berg, 2009, 8) (Gen. 2:15, 19-20; 1:26-30).

D. In essence, a man is to *procreate* with his spouse only; *govern* within the realm of authority, influence, and strength given by God; and *lead* within the realm of authority, influence, and strength given by God (Gen. 2:15; 1:26-30; 1 Cor. 11:1-3).

IV. The disciplines of manhood: Men's primary goal is not to relax but to work for the glory of God (Chanski, 2004, 49-50). Men were not called to follow the world's order but to set things in order in all aspects of life to the glory of God and the benefit of all humanity (Dewitt, 1994, 9-21).

Therefore, it is prudent for man to learn, live, and discipline himself around the precepts and plans of God (Gen. 1:27, 2:15; 1 Cor. 11:1-3; Prov. 14:8).

V. Implications for men

A. Men must manage the *people* within the garden in which God has placed them, according to the commands of God.

B. Men must maintain and manage the *possessions* within the garden in which God has placed them, according to His commands.

C. Men must maintain and manage the *property* within the garden in which God has placed them, according to His commands.

D. Men must disengage from *perpetrators* that keep them from functioning within their God-given roles as commanded by God.

E. Men must distrust *perspectives* that keep them from functioning within their God-given roles as commanded by God.

F. Men must deny *passions* that keep them from functioning within their God-given roles as commanded by God.

Key Point: A man is to think and reason in a manner that reflects maturity. "When I was a child, I used to speak like a child, think like a child, reason like a child; when I became a man, I did away with childish things" (1 Cor. 13:11). A man is to relate with people and handle circumstances in ways that demonstrate he is no longer a child. The natural tendency of men is to be domineering or passive. Men must fight against those two extremes while seeking to live according to the order set by God as they seek to set things in order as prescribed by God.

The Role of the Husband

I. Husbands are to love their wives (Eph. 5:25-31).

A. Meaning of passage—to sacrifice self for the benefit, provision, welfare of his wife in all aspects of her life (Eph. 5:25-31).
B. Member of the family—to his wife (Eph. 5:25-31).
C. Manner of service—as Christ loved the Church (Eph. 5:25-31).
D. Motive behind service—to help her become holy/blameless, so that she may function according to God's design (Eph. 5:25-31).
E. Magnitude of service—to death (1 John 3:16-18).
F. Manifestation of service—considering her interests, concerns, needs, desires, and making sure they are taken care of in the way that Christ would do this for the Church; relating with her socially, spiritually, emotionally, and sexually in a manner that benefits her and reflects the character of Christ; compensating for her weaknesses in ways that Christ would for the Church; leading and guiding her into spiritual maturity by helping her to be all that God designed her to be in the way that Christ would for the Church; leading his wife as Christ would lead the Church in all aspects of the marriage (1 Peter 3:7, 1 Cor. 7:33).

II. Example of a job description:

A. Position title: Husband (Head of Family)
B. Purpose of the position: To lead, love, feed, watch over, protect, and serve wife and those of the household (1 Cor. 11:3, Eph. 5:25-27, 1 Tim. 5:8, John 13:1-17, 1 John 3:16, Acts 20:28).
C. Reports to: Jesus Christ, elders, accountability couple
D. Relates closely with: wife, children, mother, father, mother-in-law, and father-in-law
E. Responsible for:

1. Leading the family in the direction designed by God for this family (Josh. 24:14-15).
2. Setting an example for godly living (Matt. 5:6, 1 Tim. 4:16).
3. Establishing a system for discipling the family to spiritual maturity (Eph. 5:25-27, 6:4; Heb. 10:24; Prov. 22:6; 1 Cor. 14:35).
4. Providing financial provisions to meet the basic needs of the immediate family and household (1 Tim. 5:8, 1 John 3:16-19).
5. Establishing guidelines and goals for every aspect of living in the home, according to God's standards and design for the family (1 Tim. 3:4-5).

6. Making sure each member (if Christian) of the family is connected to and serving in the local church assembly (Heb. 10:24-25).
7. Providing support and service to all members of the household, in order that they may live out the purpose God designed for each individual in the household (Rom. 12:9-13, Heb. 3:12-13).
8. Protecting the family against hurt, harm, and danger (1 John 3:16, Acts 20:28).
9. Providing sexual fulfillment to wife unconditionally (1 Cor. 7:1-5).

F. Continuing responsibilities

1. Assisting in handling household responsibilities (Phil. 2:3-4).
2. Tracking the spiritual growth of the immediate family and household (John 21:15-17).
3. Honoring, praising, and showing appreciation to his wife on a consistent basis (Prov. 31:28, 1 Peter 3:7).
4. Establishing and providing opportunities for family fun, fellowship, and travel (Acts 2:42, Heb. 10:25).
5. Seeking constantly to understand who his wife is and how to serve and honor her accordingly (1 Peter 3:7).

G. Measurable goals for the position

1. What life skills are being developed in my life and family?
2. What needs am I meeting for my wife, children, and others right now?
3. What commitments am I keeping?
4. What household responsibilities am I maintaining?
5. What social events/hobbies have we been involved in?
6. What trips have we taken?
7. What level of spiritual maturity is found in my family?
8. Whose burdens are we bearing and needs are we meeting for one another and for those outside the family?
9. What have I protected my family from?
10. What financial provisions are being made for my family?
11. How much debt are we going into?
12. How much debt are we coming out of?
13. What goals have we set and accomplished as a family and as individuals in the family?
14. What souls have been saved as a result of our family?
15. What lives have grown spiritually as a result of our family?

SECTION 24

Understanding Womanhood and the Role of the Wife

I. The definition of a female (*nâqebah* /nek·ay·baw/): one who was created by God as a material and immaterial being with a unique DNA, two X chromosomes, and the physical distinctive of a vagina, ovaries, and a uterus for a particular function and purpose in the culture. She operates alongside yet distinct from a male and all other creations of God (Gen. 1:27).

A. A female is equal in essence to a male, yet distinct and different in her form and function from a male. She is no less than a male, but is equal to a male in her creation. Her intelligence is no less than a male's but is equal to a male's in her creation. Her form and function are just as valuable to God as those of her male counterpart.

B. In most cases, women are born with a vagina, ovaries, and a uterus. In the event there is either the absence of or an addition to the normal female sexual organs, a chromosome test should verify her gender.

II. The definition of *womanhood*: the mindset, manner, and movement that all females were distinctly created and called by God to function within in all aspects of life (Gen. 2:18). God established the roles of biblical manhood and womanhood plainly in the beginning before the Fall. Nowhere in His Word does He change this order for any reason (Gen. 1:26-27, 2:15-18; 1 Cor. 11:3, 8-9, 11-12; 1 Tim. 2:12-14).

A. *ézer kenegdo*: To function in womanhood is to function as a helper who is comparable to a man in essence and being, but distinct and different from a man in form and function. To function in womanhood is to function in such a way whereby a woman embraces the fact that she is not designed to have the same function as a man, but has a different function of equal value in order to carry out her God-given assignments alongside men.

B. She carries herself in a mindset, manner, and movement that demonstrate she was designed to complement man in the carrying out of God-given assignments that could not be done to completion or done well apart from the contribution of her form, gifts, talents, abilities, skills, personality, and treasures.

III. The duties of a *female*: the duties of a female correspond with how she was created by God from the beginning to function (Gen. 2:18).

A. Women are responsible for supporting men in *procreation on earth*—carrying the life implanted through the seed of her husband to birth, so that humans would reflect the character of God throughout the earth (Gen. 1:26-28).

B. Women are responsible for supporting men in *subduing the earth*—supporting men in governing the earth (i.e., stewardship, management, control, and order) according to the will of God (Gen. 1:26-28, 2:15-18).

C. Women are responsible for supporting men in establishing *dominion over the earth*—supporting men in overseeing the earth (Gen. 1:26-28, 2:15-18).

D. In essence, women are to *procreate* with their husbands only and to *support* and *submit* to men in the governance and leadership of creation within the realm of their influence and position to the glory of God and the good of humanity (Gen. 1:26-28, 2:15-18; 1 Cor. 11:3).

IV. The deliberation to women

A. A woman is to operate in such a manner whereby her talents, gifts, abilities, and skills correspond to or complement male headship.

B. A woman was not designed to take a man's place, but to work alongside him as placed by God to do so.

C. A woman is not to operate in a manner whereby she seeks to replace or be equal to male headship, but to correspond to or complement male headship. Where she does lead over men in areas outside the church (i.e., as employer, executive, owner of a company, civic organization leader, etc.), she does so in a way that does not compromise her femininity or dishonor a man's masculinity while glorifying God in her work accordingly.

D. Therefore, it is prudent for women to learn, live, and discipline themselves around the precepts and plans of God (Gen. 1:26-28, 2:15-18; 1 Cor. 11:3,8-9, 11-12; Prov. 14:8; Rom. 12:2; 1 Tim. 4:7).

V. The direction for women

A. Women must *delight* in their position as co-heirs with men before the throne of God.
B. Women must *develop* in the precepts of God in relation to all that He has for women to do in the position and practice established for them through the created order.
C. Women must be *disciplined* in their practice of functioning within the role that God has established through the created order.
D. Women must *dismiss* the perspective that they are less than men because of the role God established for them through the created order.
E. Women must be *devoted* to promoting the position and practice ordained for them by God to other women so that God may be glorified through their position and practice.
F. Women must *discover* the pleasure that God brings to their lives as a result of living within the created order of God.

Key Point: A woman must function in such a way that she builds up her house and does not tear it down (Prov. 14:1). An atmosphere of competition and division can be formed in many homes and many churches if the understanding and definition of equality is not solely centered around and based on the Word of God. Women are every bit as capable, as precious, and as vital to the Kingdom of Christ as any man. She is not less than a man in her intelligence, function, and value. Women have been sovereignly given a role to follow just as men have been given a role to follow. The natural, fleshly tendency of women (when not walking by the Spirit of God) is either to usurp the authority of men or to overly accommodate the authority of men in the wrong way. Women must fight against these two extremes as they seek to complement male headship in the carrying out of God-given assignments through their gifts, talents, abilities, skills, personality, and treasures.

The Practice of a Wife in Marriage

I. Wives are to submit to their husbands (Eph. 5:22-24)

A. Meaning—to willingly follow the leadership of her husband; to willingly follow the instructions of her husband (Eph. 5:22-24).
B. Member—to her own husband (1 Peter 3:1-6).

C. Manner—as the Church submits to Christ the Lord; as if she were responding to Jesus Christ Himself (Eph. 5:22-24).
D. Motive—out of respect for God's design (Eph. 5:22-24).
E. Magnitude—in everything that is not sin, including preferences (Eph. 5:22-24).
F. Manifestation—following her husband's leadership and directives in all that she does in the home and outside the home as unto the Lord; following her husband's leadership and directives in the raising of the children as unto the Lord; showing respect to her husband in all aspects of the marriage as unto the Lord; managing their home in ways that are in line with her husband's leadership and directives as unto the Lord; listening to and following through on the things that concern her husband that have been requested of her as unto the Lord (Titus 2:3-5, Prov. 31:10-31, 1 Cor. 7:34, 1 Peter 3:1-6).

II. Position Title: Wife (Support of Family)

A. Purpose of the position: To support and help her husband in various ways so that he may be and do all God designed for him (Gen. 2:18-22).
B. Reports to: God, husband, church leaders
C. Relates closely with: husband, mother, father, mother-in-law, and father-in-law
D. Responsible for:

1. Submitting to her husband in every aspect of life as unto the Lord (Eph. 5:23, Titus 2:3-5, 1 Peter 3:1)
2. Helping her husband in those areas of his life where he is unable to function adequately (Gen. 2:18)
3. Meeting his needs in every aspect of the marriage (Phil. 2:3-4, 1 Peter 4:10)
4. Showing respect to her husband (Eph. 5:33)
5. Keeping the home inviting and orderly (Titus 2:3-5, Ps. 128:3, Prov. 31:27)
6. Assisting her husband in the raising of children (Titus 2:3-5, Ps. 128:3)
7. Keeping herself beautiful inside and outside (1 Peter 3:3-5)
8. Providing sexual fulfillment to her husband unconditionally (1 Cor. 7:1-5)
9. Using her skills, talents, and gifts to support her husband and family as first priority (Prov. 31:27, Ps. 128:3, Titus 2:3-5)
10. Being loyal, trustworthy, and dependable in attitude, action, and service to her husband in every aspect of the relationship (Prov. 31:10-12)

E. Measurable goals

1. In what ways am I submitting to my husband?
2. How am I using my strengths to compensate for my husband's weaknesses?
3. What needs am I meeting of my husband?
4. What ways am I showing respect to my husband?
5. Am I keeping the home inviting and orderly?
6. What ways am I helping my husband raise our children?
7. What am I doing to keep myself attractive for my husband?
8. Is my husband satisfied sexually by me?
9. What gifts, talents, skills, and resources am I using to support my husband/my family?

SECTION 25

Biblical View of Sexuality and Sexual Sin

I. Communication

A. Many people have a hard time talking about sex at one time or another.

B. Keeping silent keeps us ignorant and potentially leads to negative sexual health outcomes.

C. Lacking basic sex information also makes talking about sex even scarier. because you don't know what you don't know.

II. Perspective of sex

A. Sex must be held in high regard and preserved for the marriage bed only (Heb. 13:4).

B. Sex is more than the physical act in that it joins one to another person on a spiritual level (1 Cor. 6:13-16).

C. Sex is not the purpose of marriage, but a good marriage will provide the means for genuine sexual satisfaction (Prov. 5: 15-23).

D. Sex outside of marriage leads a person to be in conflict with God's will for his/her life (1 Thess. 4:1-8).

III. Parameters of sex

A. Sex is designed to unite man and wife together according to their corresponding differences to produce something of value between them and through them in marriage only (Gen. 1:26-27, 2:18-25; Heb. 13:4).

B. There was no other creature by which God intended man to join in sexual union with but his wife (Gen. 2:18-25).

C. Sex with any other creature or being is considered a perversion; man is not have sex with other men or any animals, or any woman that is not his wife (Lev. 18:22-23, Heb. 13:4, Rom. 1:26-27, Jude 7).

D. Sex is not for joining identical things, or just anything at all; unless sex brings corresponding differences of man and woman together in the manner ordained by God (marriage), it promotes nothing of value (Lev. 18:22-23, Rom. 1:26-27, Jude 7).

II and III based on ideas in Heimbach, 2004, 170-172.

IV. Purpose of sex

A. God designed sex for procreation (Gen. 1:26-27).
B. God designed sex so that husbands and wives may develop in oneness and companionship (Gen 2:24-25).
C. God designed sex so that husbands <u>and</u> wives may enjoy pleasure from one another in their union (Prov. 5:15-20).
D. God designed sex so that husbands and wives may develop in intimacy (Song 7:1-12).

V. Principles of sex

A. Sexual desires are God-given and are to be enjoyed with one's legal spouse (1 Cor. 7:1-5, Prov. 5:15-23).
B. Sex was designed for your partner's pleasure unconditionally (1 Cor. 7:1-5).
C. Husbands and wives are to be committed to fulfilling the sexual desires of their partner on a regular and continuous basis (1 Cor. 7:1-5).
D. Fulfillment of sexual desires should be equal and reciprocal as well as regular and continuous (1 Cor. 7:1-5).

VI. Picture of God-honoring sex

A. God-honoring sex is between husband and wife alone with the purpose of honoring God and satisfying one's spouse (Heb. 13:4, Prov. 5:15-23).
B. God-honoring sex is personal in that it promotes the value of another instead of using another as a devalued object of sexual pleasure (1 Cor. 6:13-20).
C. God-honoring sex is intimate in that it is not just a joining of bodies but a joining of souls (Gen. 2:24).
D. God-honoring sex is sacrificial in that it is giving of oneself for the pleasure of the spouse (1 Cor. 7:1-5).

Counseling Those Committing Sexual Sins

I. The <u>prohibitions</u> and perversions of sex

A. We are not to commit adultery—married persons having sexual relations outside of their own marriage (Heb. 13:4, Prov. 6:32).

B. We are not to have premarital sex—single persons having sexual relations before marriage (1 Cor. 6:15, 1 Thess. 4:3-5).
C. We are not to practice homosexuality—persons having sex with someone of the same sex (Rom. 1:24-28, Gen. 19:1-29, 1 Cor. 6:9-11).
D. We are not to practice incest—sexual relations between persons so closely related that law or religion forbids them to marry (1 Cor. 5:1, Lev. 20:11-12,14).
E. We are not to rape anyone—the unlawful and unwanted/unconsented forcing of sexual relations (2 Sam. 13: 11-15, Deut. 22:23-29, Judges 19:25, 20:3,4,12).
F. We are not to practice prostitution/harlotry—the giving or selling of one's body for sexual and/or financial profit (Prov. 23:27, Deut. 23:18, 1 Cor. 6:15-18).
G. We are not to practice voyeurism—sexual stimulation and/or arousal by watching others engaged in sexual acts (Matt. 5:28, Exodus 20:17, Phil. 4:8).
H. We are not to watch pornography—mental/visual stimulation caused by seeing sexual conduct or nakedness (Matt. 5:28, Exodus 20:17, Phil. 4:8).
I. We are not to practice exhibitionism—the self-display of the genitals without the consent of others (Rom. 13:14, Eph. 5:1-5).
J. We are not to practice bestiality—sexual contact with animals (Ex. 22:19, Lev. 18:23, Deut. 27:21).
K. We are not to practice sado-masochism—sexual excitement that is derived through personal suffering and pain; the key is the concept of a submittal to power. Sadists want to subject the victim to pain for sexual excitement. Masochists want to be subjected to the pain for sexual excitement (Gal. 5:13, Phil. 2:3-4).

Portions of the above information were based on Dr. Stuart Scott's 1999 class "Problems and Procedures"; he is a professor of Biblical Counseling at The Master's University.

II. The pitfalls to unlawful sex

A. God will judge all who have sex outside of marriage (Heb. 13:4).
B. God will judge all who use people as objects (sexually) to gratify their lust for pleasure and excitement (1 Thess. 4:4-6).
C. Those who choose to have sex outside of marriage bring about destruction on themselves (Prov. 5:1-23).
D. Those who choose to have sex outside marriage will suffer negative consequences (Prov. 6:23-35, 1 Cor. 6:12-20).

III. The <u>process</u> of repenting of unlawful sex

A. Identify, confess, and repent of all unlawful sexual activities you are or have been participating in (1 John 1:9, Prov. 28:13-14).

B. Identify what lust(s) of your heart you were trying to satisfy through the unlawful sexual activity that has become an idol (Jas. 1:14-15, Phil. 3:17-19).

C. Seek forgiveness from those individuals with whom you have been committing sexual sin (Jas. 5:16, Luke 17:3).

D. Make a commitment to please God (2 Cor. 5:9-10,15).

E. Dwell on things that are pure (Phil. 4:8).

F. Make no more provisions for future unlawful sexual activities (1 Cor. 6:12-20, 1 Thess. 4:3-8, Rom. 13:11-14).

G. Learn how to treat older men as fathers, older women as mothers, younger men as brothers, and younger women as sisters with absolute purity (1 Tim. 5:1).

H. Learn the art of worshiping God instead of your desires (John 4:23-24, Rom. 12:1-21, Heb. 13:15-16, Matt. 4:8-10).

The Way of Sexual Immorality

MARK 7:21–23 / MATT. 6:21–23 / GAL. 5:19–21

Based on concepts from Gallagher, 2001

Disposition	+ Motives	+ Triggers	= Thoughts	= Behaviors	= Avenues
Love of self Love of pleasure Mind set on flesh	Wanting the forbidden; Wanting the pleasure of sex without the commitment to a covenant of marriage; Wanting sex as a means to something else or an escape from something else	Smell/Touch Rejection Clothes/Dress Body features Movies Music Conversation Establishments/Environment Someone playing hard to get Circumstances/Situations Boredom/Loneliness Character traits Acts of kindness/service Positions of power/status Loyalty/Support in time of need Respect Disappointment/Denied a request or expectation Flirtation/Words of kindness/ Good listener Physical build-up from lack of sex	Sinful sexual fantasies Past sexual experiences Present sexual acts Future sexual plans	Masturbation Indecent liberties Voyeurism Exhibitionism Molestation Rape Incest	Pornography People Phone sex Animals Computers Strip clubs Music Sex toys Sex games TV Movies

The Way to Sexual Purity

1 Thess. 4:3-8 / Col. 3:1-5 / 1 Cor. 6:12-20

Confession of Sin	+ Repentance of Sin	+ Renew the Mind	+ Worship the Lord	+ Train in Truth	+ Serving Others
1 John 1:9 Ps. 51 Ps. 32 Jas. 5:16	Ezek. 14:1-8 2 Cor. 7:10-11 2 Tim. 2:16-27 Jas. 4:1-10 Acts 26:19-20 Prov. 28:13-14	1 Thess. 4:3-8 2 Tim. 2:15 Rom. 12:2 Ps. 119:8-11 Ps. 103 Ps. 77:11	Ps. 37 Heb. 10:19-22 Rom. 12:1 John 4:23-24 Heb. 13:10-15	2 Peter 1:1-11 1 Tim. 5:1-2 Prov. 22:3 Prov. 13:20 Prov. 25:28 2 Tim. 2:22 Rom. 6-8:39 Matt. 5:6 Gal. 5:16-26 Matt. 18:21-35 Heb.13:4 Prov. 6:20-35	Heb. 10:24-25 Titus 3:14 Gal. 6:1-2 John 13:1-17 Rom. 12:3-21 1 Peter 4:8-10 Heb. 13:16
Pride Immoral thoughts/words/deeds Selfishness Idols/Lust of the heart	Pride Selfishness Immoral thoughts/words/deeds Desires for immoral things Idols/Lust of the heart People, places, things that promote immorality Activities, TV shows, movies, music that promote immorality Blaming others for your problem	Attributes of God Wrath of God Glory of God Justice of God Love of God Promises of God Your identity in Christ God's design for relationships How to be devoted to God God's design for marriage & sex	Praise God Thank God Present your body to God Delight in God Show respect for His ways & commands Draw near to Him	Treat women who are not your wife as mothers & sisters Set up boundaries to protect you from negative influences Resist lustful cravings through the pursuit of righteousness in thoughts/words/deeds Forgive others of sin against you Spend time with wise people	Bear burdens Meet needs Fellowship with others Corporate worship Corporate prayer Proclaim truth

Understanding Sexual Sin from the Heart

Level 1: The heart (the mind, will, affections) is the control center of one's life. All that one will or will not do is determined by the heart. If the heart is not guarded, it can be seduced by:

Level 2: The flesh (indwelling sin) waging war against the heart, leading to

Self-rule—Pride, which is basically living a self-centered life

Self-righteousness—One's personal, acquired standards as the way of life and one's preferences as the only way to do things

Which will lead to:

Level 3: Covetousness—Preoccupation with serving self and satisfying self as one operates through greed; pursuit and preoccupation with satisfying natural desires outside of God's will, neutral desires outside of God's will, and naughty desires in one's life.

Which will lead to creating:

Level 4: Idolatrous lust—an operative god of existence that serves as the center of one's life to be satisfied by any means necessary, being the result of covetousness. Idolatrous lust is a lustful desire seeking to be satisfied through any idol that could be made out of people, places, products, perspectives, or pleasure.

Which explains:

Level 5: Sexual sin—an idol that is used as a means to satisfy one's hunger, hurt, or hate

A. Sexual satisfaction is pursued outside of God's guidelines and guardrails because one has a hungry soul but refuses to come to the Bread of life (Jesus Christ) to satisfy the hungry soul, thereby running to sex to fill the void (I Hunger).

B. Sexual satisfaction is pursued outside of God's guidelines and guardrails because one has a guilty conscience or pain in the heart and refuses to come to the God of Grace (Jesus Christ) to cleanse the guilty conscience or to heal the broken heart, thereby running to sex to numb the pain (I Hurt).

C. Sexual satisfaction is pursued outside of God's guidelines and guardrails because one is fearful of losing something or not getting something deemed important, and sex has become a way to calm one's fears, or sex is being exchanged in order for one to gain what one treasures to keep from losing something or not getting something that one fears may not be received (I'm Horrified).

D. Sexual satisfaction is pursued outside of God's guidelines and guardrails because one is angry with God, people, or circumstances and refuses to accept what God has allowed, to submit to what God has commanded, and to embrace God's redemptive plans in the matter, thereby running to sex as a means of punishing others and of gaining vindications or validations (I Hate).

For further detail of these concepts, read Street, Passions of the Heart.

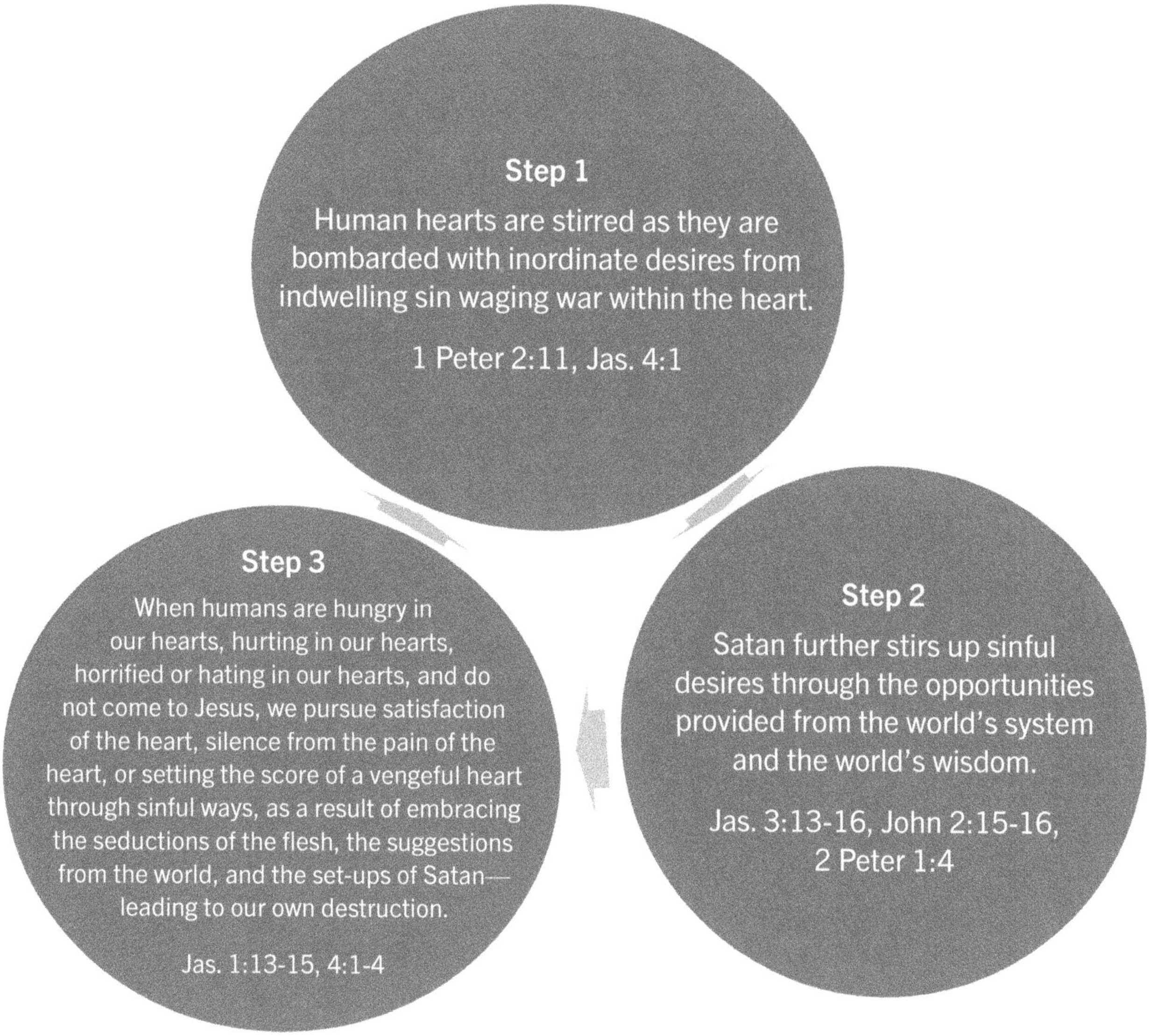

Step 1

Human hearts are stirred as they are bombarded with inordinate desires from indwelling sin waging war within the heart.

1 Peter 2:11, Jas. 4:1

Step 2

Satan further stirs up sinful desires through the opportunities provided from the world's system and the world's wisdom.

Jas. 3:13-16, John 2:15-16, 2 Peter 1:4

Step 3

When humans are hungry in our hearts, hurting in our hearts, horrified or hating in our hearts, and do not come to Jesus, we pursue satisfaction of the heart, silence from the pain of the heart, or setting the score of a vengeful heart through sinful ways, as a result of embracing the seductions of the flesh, the suggestions from the world, and the set-ups of Satan—leading to our own destruction.

Jas. 1:13-15, 4:1-4

Understanding How to Change and Redirect from Sexual Sin

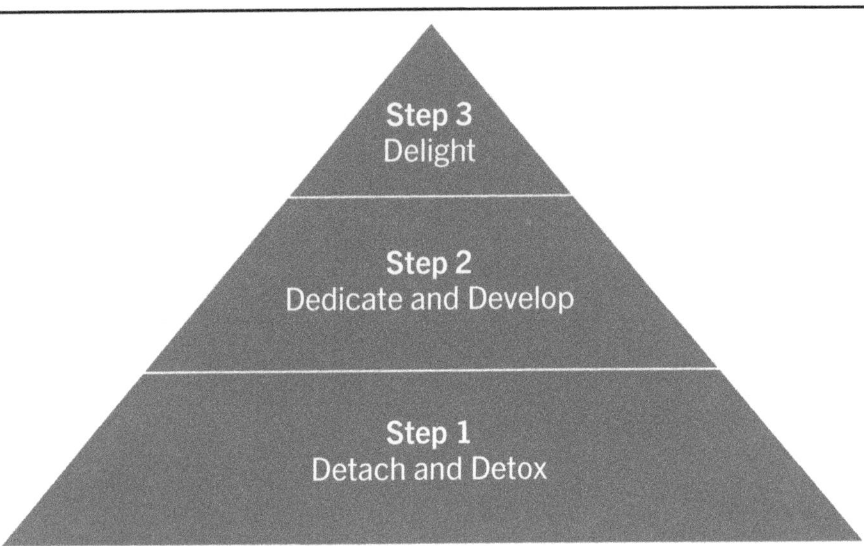

Step 1—Detach and Detox

A. **Detach**: Turn away from desires and ways of life that have captivated your heart above obedience to God (Heb. 12:1).

B. **Detox:** Learn to live with the physical pain and emotional pain that comes from detoxing, denial, disappointment, difficulty, and dishabituation (stopping a way of doing something) in relation to turning away from those desires and ways of life that have captivated your heart above obedience to God (1 Peter 4:1-2).

Step 2—Dedicate and Develop

A. **Dedicate:** Present your body as a living and holy sacrifice unto God (Rom. 12:1; 1 Peter 1:13).

B. **Develop:** Develop and persevere in Christlike character. Live with the physical pain and emotional pain that comes from the inconveniences, the afflictions, and the hardships of training in obedience to God in character and service unto the Lord in all aspects of life (Rom. 5:1-5, Jas. 1:2-4, 2 Cor. 4:7-18).

Step 3—Delight

A. **Delight**: Learn to enjoy the presence of God by embracing the characteristics of God that are most appropriate in your time of detachment, detoxing, dedication, and development.

B. **Learn to enjoy the benefits God has provided** in the present while anticipating the promises He has for you in the future in your time of detachment, detoxing, dedication, and development (Heb. 11:6; Ps. 23, 37:4).

SECTION 26

Developing Effective Communication in Marriage

Definition of communication: the transferring and receiving of information so that one may understand and respond in the proper way to the information.

I. Before we develop in effective communication, we must understand why communication was created.

A. Communication was created so that we may understand and respond properly to the *Person of God* (John 1:1-18).

B. Communication was created so that we may understand and respond properly to the *creation of God* (Gen. 1: 1-31, Ps. 19:1-6).

C. Communication was created so that we may understand and respond properly to the *commands of God* (Ps. 119:34, 73, 144).

D. Communication was created so that we may understand and respond properly to *one another* (Eph. 4:29).

II. Effective communication is tied to understanding the commonness of communication (insight from Smith, 1992).

A. Communication comes from the root word *communis*: the common and public connections shared by people.

B. Communication was not intended to be reduced to just *transmitting of facts*.

C. Communication was meant to be an involvement of people on a common and public level in the sharing of information to the building of *commonness of understanding*.

D. Tools transmit facts, but *people* get involved.

III. Effective communication is tied to understanding the control of communication.

A. Communication *reflects* what's in our *hearts* (Luke 6:44-45).

B. Communication *defines* and *interprets* our *perspective* of life (Luke 6:44-45).

C. Communication *exposes* the system of life by which we *operate* (1 John 4:5-6).
D. Communication *directs* and *shapes* our *relationships* with others (Prov. 12:18).

IV. The carelessness of listening to our spouse according to our own understanding leads to foolishness (Prov. 3:5, 28:26).

A. When we listen to our spouse according to our own understanding, we tend to interpret the conversation by our *picture* of them, allowing our opinions to determine how we listen; this leads to foolishness.
B. When we listen to our spouse according our own understanding, we tend to interpret the conversation according to our preferences, allowing what we want them to do or think in relation to the matter to determine how we listen, leading to foolishness.
C. When we listen to our spouse according to our own understanding, we tend to interpret the conversation according to our *pain*, allowing our disappointments, hurts, and frustrations to determine how we listen, leading to foolishness.
D. When we listen to our spouse according to our own understanding, we tend to interpret the conversation according to our *passions*, allowing what we want from them to determine how we listen, leading to foolishness.

V. The carefulness of listening to our spouse according to God's wisdom leads to discernment (Prov. 8:32-35).

A. When we listen to our spouse according to God's wisdom, we can seek to determine if the issue is a *matter of preference*—neither right or wrong; no moral implication; just the way our spouse prefers something to happen or to be.
B. When we listen to our spouse according to God's wisdom, we can seek to determine if the issue is a *matter of conscience*—neither right or wrong but held as a conviction by our spouse as right or wrong according to his or her personal, acquired standard.
C. When we listen to our spouse according to God's wisdom, we can seek to determine if the issue is a *matter of wisdom*—seeking to determine the good, better, or best course of action in a situation.
D. When we listen to our spouse according to God's wisdom, we can seek to determine if the issue is a *matter of sin*—a moral situation whereby our spouse is either doing what God has commanded or is disobeying what God has commanded.

Concepts based on ideas from Scott, 2005

VI. We must be cautious to listen to our spouse with the intent to gain knowledge about him or her (Prov. 18:15).

A. We should make sure we have correctly *heard* our spouse's words.
B. We should seek to understand what our spouse *means* by his/her words.
C. We should seek to understand what our spouse is *feeling* through her/his words.
D. We should seek to understand what our spouse is trying to *accomplish* through his/her words.

VII. We must consider what needs to be said in the context of a situation in order to communicate according to God's purpose to our spouse (Prov. 15:28).

A. When we are pondering how to answer, we must consider the *person* with whom we are speaking. We should ask ourselves: "What do I know about this person that should shape what I am about so say?"
B. When we are pondering how to answer, we must consider the *problem*. We should ask ourselves: "What is the real need or problem and how should I address it?"
C. When we are pondering how to answer, we must consider the *process* by which we are going to communicate. We should ask ourselves: "Will this way I'm about to go about this communication be beneficial to this person?"
D. When pondering how to answer, we must consider the *precepts* of God's Word. We should ask ourselves: "What does God's Word have to say about this?"

VI and VII above based on ideas from Tripp, 2000.

SECTION 27

Foundations for Child Rearing

I. Parents are to exercise their authority as God's agent. They are to direct their children to the glory of God and the benefit of the child. They are not to direct their children according to their personal agendas or their selfish ambitions (Eph. 6:4) (Tripp, 2021, xviii).

II. Parents are to shepherd the hearts of their children into God's wisdom. They are to help children come to understand who they are and why they do what they do. They are to teach their children who God is, how He operates, and how they are to relate to Him (Deut. 6:1-9) (Tripp, 2021, xx).

III. Parents are to lead their children to the gospel of Jesus Christ. They need to help their children understand why they need God. They are to help their children understand how and why they are slaves to sin from the inside out. Parents need to help them understand the power and purpose of the gospel in relation to their lives (2 Cor. 5:20-21, Rom. 3:1-31) (Tripp, 2021, xx).

IV. Since the heart of the child determines the behavior of a child, parents must learn the process of looking at behavior as a means of identifying what is in the heart to understand what is driving the decisions of their children (Luke 6:43-45).

V. Parents must attend to the behavior and the hearts of their children to facilitate change from the inside out. They must help children understand the connection between their hearts and their behavior and their need for Christ to save them from themselves (Prov. 20:5, Rom. 3:1-31, 2 Cor. 5:20-21).

VI. Parents must discipline and instruct their children. They must instruct them in what to do and why they do what they do. Parents must discipline and correct them when they do wrong and show them why and how they must do things God's way through a genuine relationship with Jesus Christ (Eph. 6:4) (Tripp, 2021, 4-5).

VII. Parents must help children understand that they are living a life either in rebellion or submission to Christ (Gal. 6:7-8).

VIII. Parents must help children understand that true life and satisfaction will only come through a right relationship with Christ and nothing else (John 6:26-71).

IX. Parents must evaluate their own lives before God to see where they stand and how their walk with God is influencing the life of their children (2 Cor. 13:5).

SECTION 28

Parents, Bring Them Up in the Discipline of the Lord

EPHESIANS 6:4B

I. Children are born sinners (Ps. 58:3).

II. Children have defiled hearts filled with foolishness and folly (Mark 7:17-23, Prov. 22:15).

III. If the foolishness and folly go unchecked, their behavior will express consistent foolishness and folly, which can lead to the destruction of the child (Prov. 13:15).

IV. The folly that is in a child's heart must be driven out (Prov. 22:15).

V. God tells us in His Word that the rod of correction is the means by which the folly is driven out (Prov. 22:15).

VI. God has not explained how the rod of correction removes folly. Therefore, we must trust God on the basis of what He said (Prov. 3:5-8).

VII. The Bible is very clear about the rod of correction:

A. Prov. 13:24
B. Prov. 22:15
C. Prov. 23:13-14
D. Prov. 29:15

VIII. In our use of the rod of correction, we must make a distinction between behavior that is childish and behavior that is defiant.

A. The rod is to be used for defiant (sinful) behavior and not childish, silly behavior. (We know that kids will be silly.)

B. In our use of the rod, we must never discipline children while we are in sinful anger (Jas. 1:19-20).

IX. The goal of our discipline must be out of love for God and love for our children, resulting in restoration, not retribution (Prov. 13:24, Heb. 12:5-11).

X. When we use the rod as God designed it (Tripp, 2021, 114-115):

A. *Shows God's authority over Mom and Dad*. When parents use the rod as God instructed, they show that they are following authority as they are working with their children to do the same (Luke 6:40).

B. *Trains children to be under authority.* Kids must learn that everyone is under authority and that it is far better to be submissive to authority than to be against authority (Prov. 29:15, Rom. 13:1-7).

C. *Demonstrates parental love and commitment.* Proper discipline demonstrates that parents are seeking to do what is best even if it brings pain (Prov. 13:24).

D. *May yield a harvest of peace and righteousness.* Properly administered discipline, while unpleasant and painful at the time, tends to yield disciplined, self-controlled children (Heb. 12:11, Prov. 29:17).

SECTION 29

Parents, Bring Them Up in the Instruction of the Lord

Ephesians 6:4b

I. Infancy to childhood (0 to 5 years)

A. In the first five years, the primary training objective is to teach our children to be under the authority of God (Eph. 6:1-3).

B. Children are to learn to obey authority without delay, debate, or discussion (Tripp, 2021, 138-9).

II. Childhood (5–12 years)

A. The primary training objective from 5 to 12 years is to build character.

B. Our children's character must be developed in areas such as dependability, honesty, kindness, consideration, helpfulness, diligence, loyalty, humility, self-control, and moral purity, as well as many others (Prov. 22:6) (Tripp, 2021, 163).

C. Our children need biblical wisdom in dealing with issues of the heart as well as of behavior (Prov. 4:1-13).

D. The goal at this stage is to help our children see and address issues that deal more with the ugliness in their character, such as selfishness or mocking; issues of defiance are hopefully secondary issues at this stage as a result of consistent discipline in the earlier stage of training (Tripp, 2021, 164).

III. Teenagers to adulthood

A. The primary objectives at this stage of parenting are to teach our children the fear of the Lord, adherence to parental instruction, and disassociation from the wicked (Tripp, 2021, 188).

B. Parents should seek to influence young people to respond to things based on Scripture in all aspects of their lives.

C. According to the Bible (Rom. 12:2-21, 1 Pet. 4:10-11, Eccl. 5:18-20), we want to seek to help young people to

1. Develop a Christian mind about all things (Rom. 12:2).
2. Develop relationships that are God-honoring (Rom. 12:8-21).
3. Discover and develop a ministry that accords with their giftedness (Rom. 12:3-7).
4. Discover a career in which they can fulfill the cultural mandate and God's command that they support themselves and share with others in need.
5. Establish their own home and family identity as a member of society and a part of the Body of Christ.

IV. A biblical perspective of child development

A. Children's orientation toward God will determine how they develop and the direction of their lives (Gal. 5:16-24, Gal. 6:7-8).

B. The Bible teaches that humans sin because they are sinners. Children are not an exception. Children are not morally neutral. They come from the womb wayward and sinful (Ps. 58:3, Ps. 51:5) (Tripp, 2021, 21).

C. Children either respond to God by faith or they suppress the truth in unrighteousness (Ps. 58:3) (Tripp, 2021, 20).

D. "Folly is bound up in the heart of a child, but the rod of discipline will drive it far from him" (Prov. 22:15).

E. Children are not the sum total of what we put in them. They interact with life either out of a true faith in Christ or with a life of unbelief in Christ (Rom. 8:5-14).

F. When parenting children, the parents must distinguish between immaturity and sins against God. They are not the same.

G. Immaturity is when one is speaking or acting in a way that shows a lack of development in a particular area, which may result in clumsiness or inconsistency (1 Cor. 13:11, Heb. 5:11-14).

H. Sin is when one thinks, speaks, or acts in ways that are a violation of God's will and ways (1 John 3:4-10).

I. A person can grow out of immaturity. He or she must confess and repent of sin and turn to God to be cleansed and delivered from it (1 John 1:9, Prov. 28:13-14, Heb. 5:11-14).

J. Parents will have a hard time helping their children develop unless they see their children's behavior as a reflection of hearts that are either oriented toward God or toward serving self (Gal. 5:16-25).

K. Parents must be faithful in seeking to shepherd the hearts of children in the direction of knowing and serving God, knowing they as parents have no control over the outcome of their children's lives (Col. 1:28, 2 Tim. 2:24-26).

L. When children are driven by godly principles, they will become slaves to God, which leads to genuine righteousness and eternal life in Christ (Rom. 6:21).

M. When children are driven by the flesh, they will become slaves of sin (Prov. 5:21-23).

N. Every choice that children make is driven by thoughts rooted in pleasing self or in pleasing God. Their thoughts are driven by a love of self and of pleasure or a love of God and of others. Their actions/reactions/feelings in circumstances expose the nature of their heart orientation (Prov. 23:7a, Rom. 8:5-14, 2 Tim. 3:1-9, 1 John 2:3-11).

O. When children have a heart oriented toward self, eight key characteristics will begin to manifest:

1. Their minds will be set on things below instead of things above, leading them to make self-interest a priority over God's will (Phil. 3:17-19, Jas. 3:13-4:3).
2. Their desires will become preoccupations, resulting in using people, places, possessions, and power to satisfy these desires (Ez. 14:1-3).
3. They will build their lives around these desires that have become preoccupations (Phil. 3:17-19).
4. They will become servants of their flesh to satisfy these desires that have become preoccupations (Gal. 5:16-21).
5. They will become slaves to that which they pursue (2 Pet. 2:18-19).
6. They will develop sinful habits that are hard to break (Prov. 5:21-22).
7. They will reap negative consequences of their sinful habits and idolatrous lustful pursuits (Gal. 6:7-8).
8. They will have a negative effect on the lives of those around them (1 Cor. 5:1-6).

P. We must seek to be faithful to work on leading our children into a heart oriented toward God, knowing that the outcome is not determined by us (1 Cor. 3:7-8).

1. We must identify desires or cravings that have preoccupied the minds of our children and seek to lead them to confess and repent of these things and turn to Jesus Christ for salvation (Prov. 28:13-14, John 3:16-18).
2. We must seek to help our children to replace these desires or cravings that have preoccupied their minds with attitudes, words, actions, relationship patterns, and service that glorify God (Eph. 4:17-32, Col. 3:1-25).
3. We must seek to help them make God a priority in all that they think, say, and do (1 Cor. 10:31).
4. Our desire is that there will be a change in their actions/reactions/feelings, resulting in a heart oriented toward God.

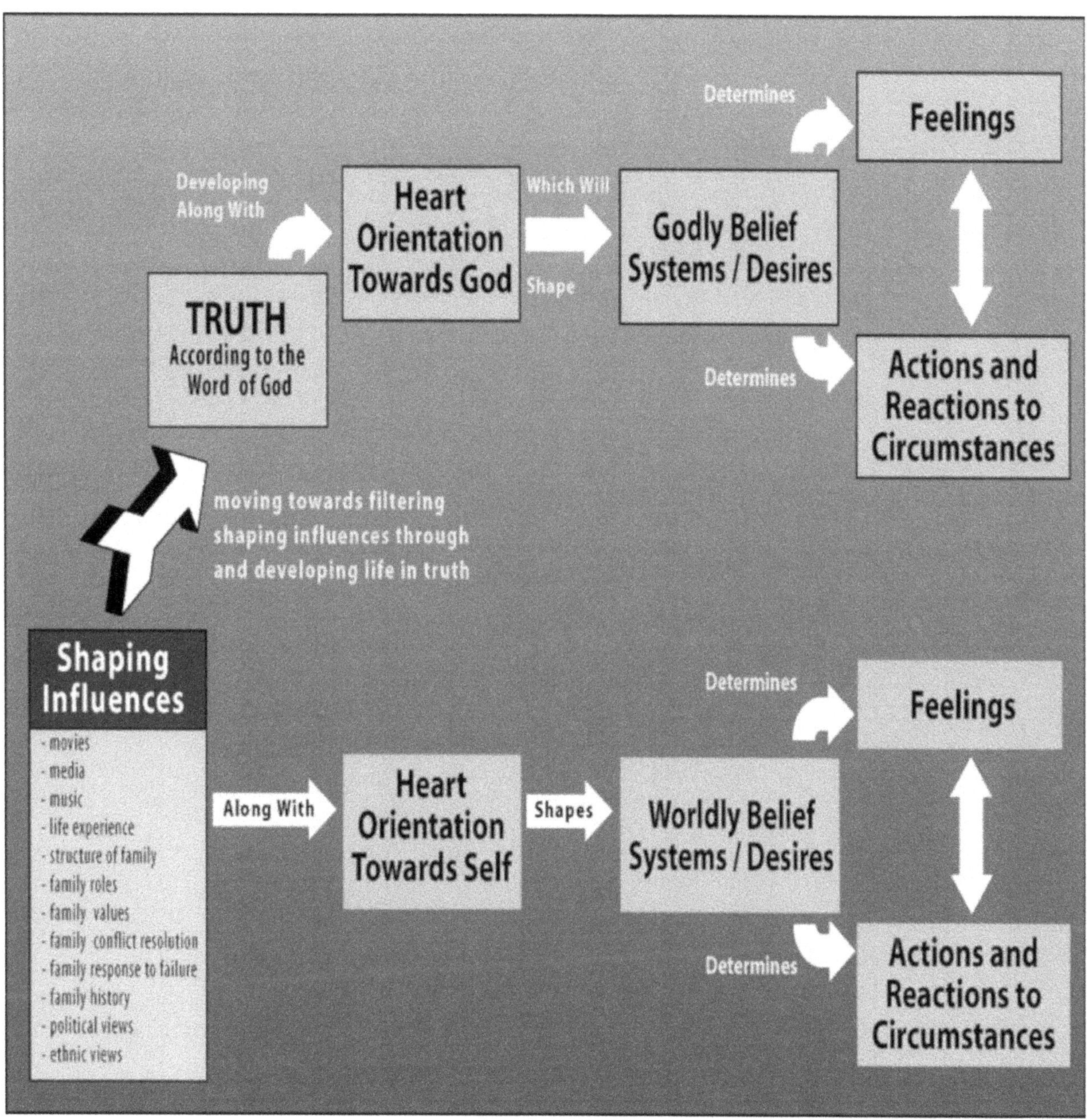

Graphic design by Adrian Baxter

BIBLIOGRAPHY AND OTHER SOURCES

Adams, Jay. *Competent to Counsel: Introduction to Nouthetic Counseling*. Phillipsburg, NJ: Presbyterian & Reformed Publishing, 1970.

————, *How to Help People Change: The Four-Step Biblical Process.* Grand Rapids, MI: Zondervan, 1985.

American Counseling Association. *ACA Code of Ethics*. Alexandria, VA: ACA, 2014.

Barcley, William B. *The Secret of Contentment.* Phillipsburg, NJ: P&R Publishing. 2010. Kindle edition.

Barry, John D., et al., eds. *The Lexham Bible Dictionary.* Bellingham, WA: Lexham Press, 2016.

Berg, Jim. *When Trouble Comes.* Greenville, SC: Bob Jones University Press, 2002.

Berger, Daniel R., II. *The Chemical Imbalance Delusion.* Greenville, SC: Alethia International Publishing, 2015.

————. *Rethinking Depression: Not a Sickness Not a Sin.* Taylors, SC: Alethia International Publications, 2019.

Boereê, Willem A. *The Integration of Psychology and Christian Faith:* 2011. http://www.ccaa.net.au/documents/CCAA-2011-73TheIntegrationofPsychologyandChristianFaith.pdf

Corey, Gerald. *Theory and Practice of Counseling and Psychotherapy*. 10th ed. Boston: Cengage Learning, 2016.

Counseling 506: Integration of Psychology, Theology, and Spirituality. Liberty University Lecture Notes, 2016. http://counseling4christians.com/Videos/IntegrationDocuments/Week%201,%20Lectures%201%202%203%20With%20S1

Dever, Mark. "Truth and Love." *Desiring God,* 2014. https://www.desiringgod.org/articles/truth-and-love

Easton, M.G. *Easton's Bible Dictionary.* Oak Harbour, WA: Logos Research System, Public Domain reprint. 1996.

Elwell, Walter A., and Philip Wesley Comfort. *Tyndale Bible Dictionary*. Tyndale Reference Library. Wheaton, IL: Tyndale House Publishers, 2001.

Erickson, Millard J. *Christian Theology*. 2nd ed. Grand Rapids, MI: Baker Academic, 1998.

"Exploring the Differences: Descriptive vs. Prescriptive Data Analytics." *AI for Beginners*. accessed August 27, 2025. https://aiforbeginners.org/exploring-the-differences-descriptive-vs-prescriptive-data-analytics

Gallagher, Steve. *At the Altar of Sexual Idolatry*. Dry Ridge, KY: Pure Life Ministries, 2001.

Heimbach, Daniel R. *True Sexual Morality: Recovering Biblical Standards for a Culture in Crisis*. Wheaton, IL: Crossway, 2004. pastordaveonline.org+14books.google.com+14amazon.com+-14time.com

Hodge, A.A. "Providence," in *Outlines of Theology*, ed. Edward N. Gross. Carlisle, PA: The Banner of Truth Trust, 1983.

Hodge, Charles. *Commentary on 1 & 2 Corinthians*. Edinburgh: Banner of Truth Trust, 1974.

Johnson, Eric L., ed. *Psychology and Christianity: Five Views*. 2nd ed. Downers Grove, IL: InterVarsity Press, 2010.

Jones, Stanton L. *Modern Psychotherapies: A Comprehensive Christian Appraisal*. Downers Grove, IL: IVP Academic, 2010.

Kim, Yong Tae. "A Christian Counseling Model: Christian Psychology Perspective," *Semantics Scholar. 2021.* semanticscholar.org.

Lambert, Heath. *The Biblical Counseling Movement After Adams*. Wheaton, IL: Crossway, 2011.

————. *A Theology of Biblical Counseling: The Doctrinal Foundations of Counseling Ministry*. Grand Rapids, MI: Zondervan, Kindle Edition, 2016.

Lightfoot, J.B. "The Epistles of St. Paul III: The First Roman Captivity." *Saint Paul's Epistle to the Philippians, A Revised Text with Introduction, Notes and Dissertations*. London: Macmillan, 1896.

MacArthur, John, and Wayne A. Mack. *Counseling: How to Counsel Biblically*. Nashville, TN: Thomas Nelson, 2005.

Mack, Wayne. *Homework Manual for Biblical Living*. Phillipsburg, NJ: P&R Publishing, 1979.

Mehl, Scott. *Loving Messy People: The Messy Art of Helping One Another Become More Like Jesus*. Wapwallopen, PA: Shepherd Press, 2020.

Piper, John. *God Is the Gospel: Meditations on God's Love as the Gift of Himself*. Wheaton, IL: Crossway, 2005.

———. "How To Get Wisdom Become a Fool," April, 2018. accessed August 11, 2018. http://www.desiregod.org/messages/how-to-get-wisdom

———. "Truth and Love." *Desiring God*, 2014. https://www.desiringgod.org/articles/truth-and-love

Powlison, David. *Speaking the Truth in Love: Counsel in Community*. Greensboro, NC: New Growth Press, 2005.

———. "The Biblical Counseling View." In *Psychology and Christianity: Five Views*, edited by Eric L. Johnson. 2nd ed. Downers Grove, IL: InterVarsity Press, 2010.

Stuart, Scott. *Communication and Conflict Resolution: A Biblical Perspective*. Bemidji, MN: Focus Publishing, 2005.

———. *The Exemplary Husband: A Biblical Perspective*. Bemidji, MN: Focus Publishing, 2002.

Smith, Donald K. *Creating Understanding: A Handbook for Christian Communication across Cultural Landscapes*. New York City: Harper Collins, 1992.

Smith, Robert D. *The Christian Counselor's Medical Desk Reference*. Bemidji, MN: Focus Publishing, 2000.

Street, John. *Passions of the Heart: Biblical Counsel for Stubborn Sexual Sins*. Phillipsburg, NJ: P&R Publishing, 2019.

Strong, Augustus Hopkins. *Systematic Theology: A Compendium and Commonplace-Book Designed for the Use of Theological Students.* Rochester, NY: Press of E. R. Andrews, 1886.

Thomson, Rich. *The Heart of Man and Mental Disorders: How the Word of God Is Sufficient.* 2nd expanded ed. Alief, TX: Biblical Counseling Ministries, 2012.

Tripp, Paul David. *Instruments in the Redeemer's Hands: People in Need of Change Helping People in Need of Change*. Phillipsburg, NJ: P&R Publishing, 2002.

————. *A Quest for More: Living for Something Bigger Than You.* Greensboro, NC: New Growth Press, 2007.

————. *War of Words: Getting to the Heart of Your Communication*. Phillipsburg, NJ: P&R Publishing, 2000.

Tripp, Tedd. *Shepherding a Child's Heart*. Updated and Expanded Edition. Wapwallopen, PA: Shepherd Press, 2021.

"What is Sanctification?" accessed November 5, 2009. http://gotquestions.org/sanctification.html

Willard, Dallas. *The Divine Conspiracy: Rediscovering Our Hidden Life in God.* New York: HarperCollins, 2009.

Wood, D.R.W., and I. Howard Marshall. *New Bible Dictionary.* Downers Grove, IL: InterVarsity Press, 1996.

Wuest, Kenneth S. *Wuest's Word Studies from the Greek New Testament: For the English Reader*. S. 1 Ti 4:7-9. Grand Rapids, MI: Eerdmans, 1997.

BIOGRAPHY

Dr. Nicolas Ellen is the Senior Pastor of Community of Faith Bible Church in Houston, Texas, and Senior Professor of Biblical Counseling at the College of Biblical Studies in Houston. Dr. Ellen is also a Visiting Professor and Co-Director of the MABC and DMin program at Central Baptist Theological Seminary in Plymouth, Minnesota. In addition, Dr. Ellen has also developed a biblical counseling training center called Expository Counseling Training Center LLC.

He received his B.A. in Business Administration from the University of Houston; his M.A. in Christian Education from Dallas Theological Seminary, Dallas, Texas; his M.A. in Biblical Counseling from The Masters University, Santa Clarita, California; his Doctorate of Ministry with a concentration in Biblical Counseling from Southern Baptist Theological Seminary, Louisville, Kentucky; and his PhD in Biblical Counseling from Southwestern Baptist Theological Seminary, Fort Worth, Texas.

Dr. Ellen is a certified Biblical Counselor with the Association of Certified Biblical Counselors (ACBC), a Fellow with the Association of Certified Biblical Counselors (ACBC), and travels nationwide with the organization teaching biblical counseling principles. Dr. Ellen and his wife, Dr. Venessa Ellen, have two children and four grandchildren.

www.ingramcontent.com/pod-product-compliance
Lightning Source LLC
Chambersburg PA
CBHW040839300326
41935CB00046B/1851

* 9 7 8 1 9 5 2 9 0 2 1 0 9 *